WHO NEEDS DRAMA?

WHO NEEDS DRAMA?
A Resource for Teaching Primary and Junior Drama

Jackie Bennett

Rock's Mills Press
Rock's Mills, Ontario • Oakville, Ontario
2024

The author is available to give workshops on drama, and can be contacted through the publisher at customer.service@rocksmillspress.com

Published by
Rock's Mills Press
www.rocksmillspress.com

Copyright © 2024 by Jackie Bennett.
All rights reserved. No part of this publication may be reproduced, distributed, or transmitted in any form or by any means, including photocopying, recording, or other electronic or mechanical methods, without the prior written permission of the publisher, except in the case of brief quotations embodied in critical reviews and certain other noncommercial uses permitted by copyright law. For permission requests, including reprints of the plays included in the book, contact the publisher at customer.service@rocksmillspress.com

Editing: Amanda Shaw
Formatting: Fe Ong-ongowan

DEDICATION

DOREEN KENNEDY was my first drama teacher during a time in my life where I knew little about the theatre. Five years of her classes not only gave me a rich knowledge of everything on and off stage but inspired me to study drama at university and then go on to teach drama in schools, direct musicals, write and produce a play, and finally to write *Who Needs Drama?* She passed away before I could tell her that because of her passion for theatre the roads in my life have continually led me back to the stage. I dedicate this book to her.

CONTENTS

INTRODUCTION
    Who Needs Drama?   1
CHAPTER ONE
    The Overall Drama Program   5
CHAPTER TWO
    The Creative Process (From Brainstorming to Performing)   7
CHAPTER THREE
    The Elements of Drama   11
CHAPTER FOUR
    Cultural Representation   13
CHAPTER FIVE
    Drama Forms   15
CHAPTER SIX
    Developing the Student Critic   19
CHAPTER SEVEN
    Who Is This For?   21
CHAPTER EIGHT
    Creative and Dramatic Play   23
CHAPTER NINE
    Helping Students Build Confidence when Performing   27
CHAPTER TEN
    Integrating Drama with the Rest of the Curriculum   33
CHAPTER ELEVEN
    Lesson Plans   37
CHAPTER TWELVE
    Acting   47
CHAPTER THIRTEEN
    One-Act Plays   51
CHAPTER FOURTEEN
    Drama Games   55
CHAPTER FIFTEEN
    Putting on a Play   61
CHAPTER SIXTEEN
    Starting a Drama Club   77
CHAPTER SEVENTEEN
    Before the Curtain Closes   79
CHAPTER EIGHTEEN
    Drama Ideas for Lessons Based on the Drama Curriculum   81
INDEX   133
Peer Changer   137
The Baseball Cap   150
Spiders, Dogs and Underwear   165
The Time Machine   177
Working Together to Save the Environment   199
SOURCES   215

INTRODUCTION
Who Needs Drama?

Who needs drama? No one, if we're talking about the kind of drama that has someone screaming at the neighbours while throwing things out a window. But purposeful creative drama is another story. Drama gives students the opportunity to develop skills that will benefit them academically and throughout their life. And yet it is often overlooked in schools either due to budget cuts or because it is not considered an essential part of the curriculum.

One of the current priorities in education is to develop the whole student. This includes intellectual, physical, emotional, creative, and social dimensions. If you were told of a new subject that would develop all these aspects of a student's educational and emotional development, would you be interested? If you were told there already is such a subject and that subject is drama, would you still be interested? Would you be surprised to learn that there are at least thirty benefits to learning drama?

Some of these benefits are listed below.

INTELLECTUAL BENEFITS
Students can:
- develop an understanding of situations familiar or unfamiliar to themselves while working on a play;
- learn to speak clearly and effectively in a variety of situations;
- improve concentration;
- develop written communication skills such as writing, planning, researching, editing, evaluating, etc.;
- develop verbal and nonverbal communication skills;
- enjoy opportunities to learn with different styles and developmental levels;
- use drama to enhance their learning and presentations in other subjects;
- develop listening and observational skills.

PHYSICAL BENEFITS
During drama studies, students can:
- expand their understanding of others through imitating movement;
- use their whole body when developing characters;
- communicate using their bodies and voices for different purposes and various situations.

EMOTIONAL BENEFITS
Students can:
- develop self-awareness;
- learn about their feelings and how to express them appropriately;
- learn to cope with and appropriately work through emotional and social challenges;
- develop feelings of success;
- build self-esteem and acceptance.

INTRODUCTION

CREATIVE BENEFITS
Students will:
- use the creative process to develop their dramatic works;
- learn to use a range of communication styles;
- discover problems have more than one solution;
- inspire others to deal with their unique situations;
- develop and expand their imaginations using creative thinking;
- learn the difference between creative and dramatic play.

SOCIAL BENEFITS
Students can:
- improve their social skills;
- develop an understanding and compassion for people with mental illness or physical disabilities;
- learn about the people around them, as well as people from other cultures and different time periods;
- develop teamwork, leadership, and risk-taking;
- improve their public speaking skills by learning to speak clearly, confidently and expressively;
- explore personal and global issues to gain an understanding of others;
- learn to identify and understand different points of view and therefore develop empathy and respect for others;
- explore in a safe environment social and personal issues such as bullying and racism;
- learn about cultural diversity while avoiding stereotypes or generalizations.

Why drama? It can be a hard sell to teachers who are not arts orientated. After all, there are many other subjects to teach and only a limited amount of time. Teachers give a number of reasons why they don't like to teach drama.

Some of these reasons include:
- Drama takes away from time better spent on the "important" subjects such as language and math.
- Drama doesn't serve a purpose in preparing students for life as reading and math do.
- Teachers don't know how to teach the arts.
- Teachers don't want to act in front of a class.
- Drama classes are too noisy and can quickly get out of control.

These are all valid concerns, at least to some extent, but drama does serve a valuable purpose in the educational system. Students not only learn about theatre but also about themselves and others, something which helps prepare them for life.

This book will help you understand the place of drama in the curriculum, suggest how to integrate drama into other subject areas, provide a large number of lesson plans and ideas for drama activities, and, in general, show how valuable a drama program can be.

INTRODUCTION

WHAT GOOD IS DRAMA BEYOND ENTERTAINMENT?

Drama beyond school is not just for those who want to pursue an artistic career. Theatre provides employment, generates economic activity (for instance, restaurants in theatre districts), and attracts tourists. Then there are the jobs that make use of skills honed in drama, including therapists, politicians, video game developers, teachers, ministers, sales people, and so on.

Here is a challenge: Think of a job that doesn't require drama skills. Every job interview requires you to think on your feet and speak with confidence. Every job requires you to behave in keeping with the position, to get along with co-workers, to deal with emergencies, etc. Many employees need to give presentations or reports. And everyone at some point, either at work or in their personal lives, will need to be with people they would not usually choose to spend time with. All of these situations make use of skills that are developed in a drama program.

Drama has many benefits that will help students learn to be successful and confident. Add some drama to your school day!

CHAPTER ONE
The Overall Drama Program

When planning your drama program, start with the academic curriculum from your province or state as each jurisdiction's curriculum is different (and offers excellent suggestions and ideas). *Who Needs Drama?* combines elements from various curricula.

A balanced drama program will include the use of the creative process (chapter 2), the elements of drama (chapter 3), and drama forms (chapter 5) to develop dramatic works using a wide range of sources, including personal experiences, books, other subjects, and prior learned knowledge.

GRADE 1 TO 3

The beginning of the drama journey for students in the primary grades focuses on the student's personal experiences in their immediate world as well as developing physical, academic, and creative skills. Drama experiences will emerge from what they have observed at home or through various media forms. The dramatic works created in these grades serve a variety of purposes and develop skills such as, listening, co-operating, and role-playing.

Some of the specific areas of focus are listed below.

Students will:
- use the creative process to plan, create and present short drama works for a variety of audiences;
- analyze, reflect, and respond to dramatic works they have created or observed, and use those thoughts to improve their own works;
- use the elements of drama in various dramatic works;
- develop cultural understanding by using various theatre forms;
- learn about people's lives and the communities they live in;
- see other points of view, leading to a better understanding of others;
- look for positive and constructive ways to solve everyday problems;
- learn the difference between real and imaginary play.

GRADE 4 TO 6

In the junior grades the drama journey continues. Students build on the skills they learned in the primary grades, with an emphasis on developing dramatic works more extensively. Lessons extend beyond the individual to understanding others and their points of view in order to help students solve real-life problems and build compassion and empathy for others.

Some of the specific areas of focus are listed below.

Students will:
- build on the drama skills developed in Grade 1 to 3;
- use the creative process to create a variety of short dramatic works for specific audiences and purposes;
- respond to creative works by others and themselves;
- use elements of drama in dramatic works;
- learn to stay in role/focus;
- learn about various theatre forms from their communities and other cultures, both in the present and past;

- use technology to enhance dramatic works;
- participate in dramatic and role play to develop an understanding of how others feel and to explore solutions to social challenges.

CHAPTER TWO

The Creative Process (from Brainstorming to Performing)

The nature of creativity is to freely follow your inner inspiration with no restraints. However, there are guidelines that can assist students at the beginning of their creative journey, especially with younger students who are still exploring what their particular creative skills and interests are. Just as we model how to do long division we also can model how to create something. The creative process, whether in a group or independently, can be used for anything; writing a story, choreographing a dance, drawing a picture, planning a science project etc. For this book, the focus will be on how the creative process relates to the drama curriculum.

Throughout the provinces, variations of the creative process are taught in school as part of the drama curriculum. Some curricula break this down into fewer or more stages, but the outcome is still the same. For this book, five stages are used.

The five stages of the creative process are:
1. Developing creative ideas
2. Planning
3. Practicing
4. Performing or sharing your work
5. Analyzing and reflecting on your work

1. DEVELOPING CREATIVE IDEAS

A. State the purpose and expectations
At the beginning of a new assignment or concept teachers will:
- begin by stating the goal of the assignment. For example, create a one-minute play with the words 'yes' and 'no';
- introduce a new concept by modelling an example for the students;
- tell students how long they have to work on a project;
- state the assessment expectations. Will the students be marked? What curriculum expectation will be assessed?

B. Brainstorming
The steps for brainstorming are:
- Make a list of all ideas for the given assignment. At this point, any idea, no matter how irrelevant or crazy, should be written down. These can lead to ideas for later projects.
- From the brainstorming list pull out the main ideas or themes.
- Choose from the list which main idea will be developed.
- While continuing to brainstorm, list all the ideas for achieving the main idea.
- Write a one-line synopsis of the project, e.g. "This play is about a snake that helps a thief learn that stealing is not right."
- Give the project a working title such as "The Biker Snake" which can be changed at any time but helps give an identity to the project.

2. PLANNING

Once the main and supporting ideas for the project have been decided students will start planning how this will be implemented. Some of the things to consider depending on the type and size of the project are:

- What drama form will be used? Will it be a puppet show, a skit, dance, play?
- What will the genre be? Will it be a comedy or thriller?
- What characters are needed to achieve the purpose?
- When working on a group project make sure there is the right number of parts in the drama work for each person in the group. If enough parts can't be created, consider assigning roles such as director, costume designer etc.
- What is the location? Where and when does it take place?
- Who is the target audience and where will it be performed?
- How long will it be?
- How much practice time is there? If there is only one period to work on it, then it needs to be simple and easy to develop.
- Will costumes, set, props, etc. be used?
- Where can research information be found?

3. PRACTICE

A. Experiment
Try out the various ideas. Eliminate those that don't work.

B. Creating the first draft
Create the first draft just as you would when writing a story. If a script isn't needed students can use point form to organize their ideas.

C. Rehearse
Practice what has been created. This provides the opportunity to see what works and doesn't work and allows actors to become more confident in their roles.

D. Revisions: Second draft
Share the drama work with another group, or the class, for opinions and feedback. Take the opinions offered and where appropriate, make revisions to make the drama work stronger.

4. PERFORMING OR SHARING YOUR WORK

Drama needs to be performed in order to share it with others. When performing, share the work with the intended audience with costumes and set, entrances and exits, and no stops or breaks. Whether a dramatic work is being presented for parents who have bought tickets or classmates during class time, it should always be treated as a real performance.

5. ANALYZING AND REFLECTING

This step involves using the critical analysis process, a term used in many areas of the curriculum, not just the arts. It's a form of "What do you think?" and "How can you make it better?" Students will reflect on what they, or someone else, have created and offer feedback with the intent of improving current works as well as future projects.

Using the critical analysis process will help students to:

- develop an appreciation for other people's works;

- evaluate their own and other's works critically and sensitively;
- make personal connections;
- share and explain their point of view.

The critical analysis includes:
1. Responding/ first impression
2. Analyzing
3. Review
4. Reflecting

1. RESPONDING/FIRST IMPRESSION
The first impression is the initial overall reaction to a performance or dramatic work. How did the work make you feel and how will you use what you have created or seen to improve your own work? There is no right or wrong answer as long as you can back up your response knowledgeably and are not giving inappropriate or disrespectful feedback.

Possible Question: What did you think of the play "The Wizard of Oz"?

An Answer: It made me feel sad because it made me remember what it's like to have to leave your friends behind like Dorothy has to do at the end.

An Inappropriate Answer: It made me feel hungry because it was a long play and I didn't have lunch. I thought it would be better if Dorothy went to Oz in a spaceship 'cause then she could have flown home faster.

A Disrespectful Answer: I thought the play was stupid. I didn't like it and found it boring.

Other possible questions to encourage responses could be: What does the play remind you of? How does it make you feel? Does anything confuse you? What things did the playwright do to make his point? What could make the play stronger? What things might you like to try using in your next play?

2. ANALYZING
Students talk about what they saw and discuss various aspects of the drama work using prior knowledge and experience to back up their opinions and observations.

Possible questions to answer:

What elements of drama were used? Why do you think they were used? How did the artist do that? Did it work?

3. REVIEW
Students summarize their impressions of their own or other's work.

4. REFLECTING
Reflecting on the finished project helps students improve their work for the next performance and learn from the positives and negatives for their next work.

Questions that can be asked when reflecting are: Was my play successful? What did people like? What didn't work the way I intended? What did I learn from the experience and what can I do to improve?

All these questions can be asked and answered differently by each job position involved in a drama work. For example, if a play was written and produced, the question, "Was the play successful?" could be answered in these ways:

Playwright: Based on the audience reaction the overall play was a success. The third scene in Act 2 needs some editing as people didn't laugh as much as I had expected.

Director: The third scene in Act 2 moved slowly because the actors took too long to get on stage. This took away from the intended humour of the scene.

Set Designer: The set functioned well, and there were no issues moving from one scene to the next.

Actor: The first scene went well except I wasn't expecting people to laugh so hard. I need to be prepared for that next time, so I don't lose my concentration.

Audience: The play was great. It was very funny and the time just flew by. I would recommend it to others.

The creative process can take as much time as needed. The steps outlined above can take years to complete for large projects or can take thirty minutes for a quick exercise. Students also don't need to begin at the same point in the process for each assignment. If students have just watched a performance, they can start at stage 5 to evaluate and reflect on what they can do to create a similar or better piece of work. Or if they are writing a play but won't be performing it, then they only need to follow step 1 and 2.

There are many ways for teachers to help students develop creativity. Some of these things are:

- Throughout the entire creative process, the teacher can circulate from group to group to offer appropriate guidance where needed.
- It's sometimes hard to be creative when someone is watching your every move. Teachers should be available to offer guidance but also should give students time to create on their own.
- After each new concept is taught and completed allow students a chance to create their own project based on whatever elements they would like to use.
- Provide a safe environment where students feel comfortable being creative. (See Chapter Nine for more suggestions.)
- Provide necessary materials and resources to complete the assignment.
- Resist the urge to take over. Offer guidance when necessary but allow students to be the ones to create while following their instincts.
- Provide enough time for students to finish their creations as they need the satisfaction and pride in producing a finished work.

CHAPTER THREE
The Elements of Drama

The elements of drama are the key components used when developing and understanding dramatic works. In earlier grades, the understanding and implementation of these elements will be simple, but as students progress through school, these concepts will become more complex.

(For this chapter the term "play" refers to all dramatic works, whether a thirty-second improvisation, a script, role play or full-length play.)

The five basic elements of drama used when teaching the curriculum are role or character, relationship, time and place, tension, and focus and emphasis.

ROLE OR CHARACTER
This refers to a character being played and making that part believable. This includes the following:

- **Understanding a character:**
  Who are they? Why do they behave the way they do? What are their personality traits? etc.

- **Creating or portraying the character:**
  What do they look like? How do they move? What is their voice like? Do they have any physical gestures or facial expressions unique to them? What would they wear?

- **Thinking beyond the script:**
  Making connections between a role being played and an actor's real-life experiences make a stronger characterization. (For more details on this see Chapter Twelve.)

RELATIONSHIP
Relationship explores how the character relates and responds to the other characters or situations in the play.

Some questions to help define relationship are:
- What is a character's direct relationship to the other characters? i.e. brother, colleague, friend, stranger, etc.
- How do they feel about other characters in the play? How does this reflect in their performance?
- What is the character's contribution to the story? Are they the main character? Do they bring insight to a problem? Do they bring comic relief?
- How does the personality, body language, voice, etc. of a character change when coming into contact with other characters?

TIME AND PLACE
Time and Place establishes and demonstrates the time, year, and location of when and where a play takes place.

This can be achieved through the following:

Dialogue
A character gives clues to the time and place through dialogue without necessarily stating the obvious. For example:
- Obvious: "I love being at the amusement park. I'm so glad we came here today."
- Implied: "I don't know why my parents make me come here. I always feel sick on roller coasters."

Costumes
Because fashion is representational of changes throughout history, costumes are the easiest way to demonstrate a period of time.

Set and Scenery
The style of furniture, backdrops, decor, etc. all can show where and when a play takes place.

TENSION

Tension is the atmosphere created through the script and characterization that leads to the climax of the story.

Tension can be developed by the following:

Script
A carefully written script will create tension through the dialogue and silent actions. "Two friends burying a body in silence is much more compelling than two friends talking about that time they buried that guy." —Stephen Spotswood.

The climax is the part of the story where a crisis or problem is solved and usually occurs near the end. Everything should lead to the climax. If the story wanders or reaches the climax too early, there is no tension.

Acting
An actor has a vital role in providing tension by portraying their character in such a way that helps to build the tension.

For example, if a character is about to rescue her dog from a bully, tension will be created depending on how the scene is portrayed. If the actor walks onto the stage, and says, "Leave my dog alone," picks it up and walks off there is no tension. If she hides behind a rock looking scared, takes a deep breath, walks up to the bully shaking, and whispers, "Leave my dog alone" and bravely takes her dog away, tension has been created.

Tempo
Tempo can be created through dialogue or by the actor. Slow down the dialogue or action, and it develops suspense. Speed it up, and you can create anger and tension.

FOCUS AND EMPHASIS

The script and the elements need to continually support the main idea or purpose of the dramatic work. Staying on track is key to not only keeping the audience engaged but also in helping them understand the meaning of the play.

The focus also relates to where the audience's attention is being directed. For example, if a character is looking under a couch that is where the focus is.

Ideas on how to develop the elements of drama can be found in Chapter Eighteen.

CHAPTER FOUR

Cultural Representation

By including cultural representation in a drama program, students will learn to understand and appreciate cultural differences. With global migration at a high, it is common to have a diverse mix of ethnic backgrounds in schools, providing a wealth of first-hand cultural knowledge that can be shared among students.

Cultural representation as part of a drama program is important because:

- it promotes inclusiveness;
- it celebrates diverse backgrounds;
- it develops empathy and understanding;
- it helps students to understand a variety of drama forms;
- it helps develop global leadership;
- it helps the actor and playwright develop authentic characterizations and scripts.

There are many ways to integrate cultural representation into a drama program. Some of these ways are:

- ### Classroom resources
  With today's global market it is easy to have a variety of books, posters, toys, games, etc. in the classroom that reflect diverse cultural backgrounds. These resources enable students from different backgrounds to feel included as well as learn about others.

- ### Theatre connections
  Students can use examples of theatre forms, stage designs, plays, symbols, etc. from various cultures and historical backgrounds when learning about and creating dramatic works.

  Social and cultural experiences explored through drama help students to better understand the people around them, both now and in the past. Why did playwrights and actors in the past or from different countries write or perform the way they did? Are Sophocles' messages still relevant today? How do we know we have correctly interpreted a dramatic work? These are some of the questions that can be explored through drama.

- ### Casting for plays
  When casting for plays avoid stereotyping. The prince and princess do not need to be Caucasian with blond hair and blue eyes. The evil witch does not need to have long black hair. Unless you are doing a period play about a cotton plantation, servants do not need to have dark skin or speak with an accent. Casting based on ability and suitability rather than appearance will lead to a more vibrant and culturally diverse interpretation of a play.

- ### Cultural days
  Having a culture day is a fun way for students to learn about other cultures.

The program can be as simple as giving presentations in the classroom to having an all-day special cultural event, complete with food, dancing, plays etc. Ideas on how to create cultural days can be found in cultural presentations in Chapter Ten.

- Avoid stereotypes and clichés
 When incorporating cultural diversity into dramatic works students should be encouraged to avoid stereotypes and clichés. For example, characterizations such as tall African American basketball players, British people with snobby upper-class accents, Italian men expecting women to do the housework, brainy Chinese students, etc. These are all stereotypes and not representative of how all people in a culture are.

CHAPTER FIVE

Drama Forms

Drama forms is a broad term that describes different methods and styles used to present a dramatic work, the way actors play their part, and the development of themes. It also can include genres such as comedy, musicals, horror, Greek drama, etc. In the primary/junior curriculum the focus is mainly on the way a story is presented.

The types of drama forms can be broken down into four main categories: movement, improvisation, voice, and behind the scene. Although there are other forms, these are the ones most frequently used in primary/ junior drama programs.

MOVEMENT
Within the category of movement are drama forms that use the body and face to tell a story. The most common ones are:

Clowning
Clowning is acting out situations in a comical way without speaking along with the use of colourful costumes and make-up with a fixed expression.

Dance
Dance is movement that tells a story using the whole body while moving to music.

Mask
Because a mask hides the face, an actor relies on using the physical expression of their body to tell a story. The features of the mask are created to portray a particular character type or emotion. Often a narrator tells the story as actors wearing masks do not typically speak.

Drama Forms (Photo: Jackie Bennett)

Mime
Mime is communicating a story where the actor performs without speaking, instead relying on facial expressions and body language to communicate.

Tableaux
When a group of actors freeze in position to represent a scene without speaking this is called a tableau.

IMPROVISATION
Improvisation is any dramatic performance that is unscripted and unrehearsed.

Improvisation
Improvisation is an impromptu performance that has no script and has not been rehearsed. Actors will perform on the spot, creating a scene as they go along. Emphasis is on the moment with no conclusion necessarily obtained.

Role Play
During role play, students act the part of different characters in situations they may not normally experience in order to see multiple points of view and to problem solve sensitive situations. Role play, even when brainstorming occurs first, is classified under improvisation as it does not usually use a script.

VOICE
Voice, as a drama form, includes all dramatic works where the emphasis is on vocal expression to tell a story.

Choral Reading
Choral reading is the reading of a poem, story, etc. in unison by a group of actors where all their voices blend together to sound like one voice.

Monologue
A monologue is a long speech that is delivered by one character without any interruptions.

Reader's Theatre
An actor reads a script using their voice to tell a story without costumes, props, or movement.

Songs
Lyrics are sung to tell a story.

Soundscape
A soundscape is the telling of a story with few or no words relying on sound effects to create a story or situation.

Story Telling
Story Telling is the form of telling a story out loud for an audience using facial expressions, voices, gestures, etc. to help with the interpretation of the story.

Musicals and Operas
Musicals and operas tell stories with music. Although the whole body is used in performances, the emphasis is on the interpretation of the words and emotions through the voice.

BEHIND THE SCENE
All drama forms where the actor is not seen or that use technology to tell a story come under the heading of behind the scene.

Movie and television
Stories that are presented using technology are considered behind the scene as actors are not present when an audience views the show.

Puppetry
When puppets are used to tell a story traditionally the actor providing the voices and operating the puppets is not seen.

Radio
Stories told on the radio, either live or pre-recorded, are listened to by an audience outside of the station. As the actor/ speaker is not seen content relies heavily on vocal expression, sound effects, and music to portray the story.

CHAPTER SIX
Developing the Student Critic

In the theatre world, a critic is a qualified expert who writes a published review of a performance they have attended. In the classroom, students are the critics, either reviewing their own or others' dramatic works. When taking on the role of a critic a person is expressing a knowledgeable opinion on what they have read, seen, or performed and is part of the analyzing and reflecting component of the creative process discussed in Chapter Two.

People will react differently to feedback. If someone looks at a painting and says, "I don't like how you painted the cow," an artist will respond according to their personalities and confidence level.

- Artist 1 may think, "I don't care because it means something to me."
- Artist 2 may think, "Mmm, OK, maybe the red dots on the cow's back do give the wrong message, and I should change that."
- Artist 3 might rip up their painting and run away in tears never to pick up a brush again.

It is therefore important when offering opinions that it is delivered in such a way that it is not perceived as negative but rather as constructive and supportive. Students need to be taught how to do this.

TEACHING PEER CRITIQUING

The process for teaching peer critiquing is a gradual process that continues throughout the entire Grade 1 year with reminders needed over the following years of study. This process will not only guide students to be thoughtful critics but will also help build their confidence when receiving feedback.

1. Begin by reading a story such as "Alice The Artist" by Martin Waddell in which the main character deals with people's opinions of their work.
2. Brainstorm with the class at the beginning of the year rules for appropriate critiquing and feedback. (See Chapter Nine for suggestions.) Post in the classroom a list of the most important ones.
3. Introduce critiquing slowly and gently by:
    - giving students the chance to perform a few improvisations, role plays, etc. before giving feedback so students can adjust to being in front of their peers without worrying about how they will be assessed;
    - modelling appropriate feedback after the first few performances before students take on the critic role themselves;
    - starting with emotional feedback and then gradually going beyond the emotional response of "I like it" to include knowledgeable feedback;
    - keeping an eye on your sensitive students as it can be challenging for them to hear something needs improvement.
4. Alternate between verbal feedback, whether as a class or small group, to written feedback so students aren't always being evaluated in front of their peers.
5. For older students encourage more knowledgeable feedback than emotional.

6. Use a technique such as 'two stars and a wish' to encourage a good mix of positive and constructive feedback.

DEVELOPING THE CRITIC
Once students have learned how to give sensitive feedback, there are steps to developing their ability to critique in a meaningful and constructive way. These steps are:

1. Emotional feedback
Begin with emotional responses. A good place to start, especially with younger students, is to ask: How did that make you feel? Did you like it? Would you recommend it to others? etc. Most of these questions will receive short answers. This is meant as a starting to point to encourage students to express their opinions.

2. Moving beyond yes and no
Most people have at some point asked a child, "How was your day?" and received a short "fine" in reply. Or "What did you do today?" "Nothing." To move beyond this kind of answer, guiding questions need to require more than one-word answers. "Did you like the play?" is good for a straight emotional response but to get a deeper response re-word the question to something like, "What was your favourite part of the play?" "What was the funniest part?" etc.

3. Knowledgeable feedback by making connections
Most students in earlier grades will have few live theatre experiences. However, they can make connections between:
- their work and that of their classmates;
- their personal experiences from home or their community;
- television shows, videos, and movies.

Students in the junior grades can make connections between:
- areas listed above;
- theatre productions seen in school or outside of school.

4. Knowledgeable feedback using learned skills
The final step in developing critiquing and analytical skills is being able to provide feedback based on the skills and terminology they have been learning. From Grade 4 onwards students should be able to do this comfortably with fewer leading questions from the teacher.

INTERPRETATION
Interpretation, as part of offering a critique, is giving an opinion of what the meaning of various aspects, or the whole, of a creative work is. This is an advanced concept for the primary division and even for many junior students. It is more of a focus for older students. However, junior level students should be able to offer simple interpretations. For example, "The song is about anger because the songwriter used loud instruments, the tempo was fast, and the singer shouted the lyrics."

Students should be reminded that even when giving their interpretation along with good supporting evidence, that doesn't mean the interpretation agrees with what the artist had intended.

CHAPTER SEVEN
Who Is This For?

Before a created dramatic work is begun, the intended audience needs to be determined. Ask the simple question, "Who is this for?" In many cases, the audience will be the students in the classroom, and therefore there will not be lengthy decisions needed as to the appropriateness of content. However, when a dramatic work is being planned for outside of the classroom more consideration regarding content is required.

Once the question, "Who is this for?" has been answered there are key things to be considered depending on the audience. These are:

- **Age-appropriate content**
  All content is not appropriate for all ages and therefore the age of the audience needs to be considered before beginning the creation of a dramatic work. A Halloween play about ghosts and haunted houses will be scary for students in Kindergarten. A play about sharing may be boring for students in Grade 8. Although themes like bullying are universal, topics such as sexting are not appropriate for younger audiences.

- **Appropriate vocabulary**
  Vocabulary and language used in a play should be at the same level of knowledge as the audience. Using advanced vocabulary that is difficult for younger students to understand or writing a play in Chinese about Chinese New Year for students who don't speak the language will lead to a restless audience who might not understand what the presentation is about.

- **Length of the drama work**
  Shorter presentations will hold the attention of younger audiences whereas longer works are more appropriate for an older audience.

- **School policies**
  When writing dramatic works that are to be read or performed in a school setting, policies of the school such as no swearing or violence should be adhered to.

ADAPTING ONE IDEA TO MAKE IT SUITABLE FOR DIFFERENT AUDIENCES
With modification, many drama works can be performed for more than one audience. This can be done by changing the vocabulary, using props and visual aids, or using age-appropriate examples related to the topic. Activities to learn how to write for different audiences can be found in Chapter Eighteen and Chapter Eleven.

CHAPTER EIGHT
Creative and Dramatic Play

Creative play and dramatic play are both methods that help develop imagination and lead to the understanding of others. Students begin with creative play as part of the Kindergarten curriculum, and gradually evolve into using dramatic play in higher grades. Both are an important component of a student's development and are part of the drama program.

The two forms of play are similar. Creative play is the process of a child making up pretend situations as they play with their toys. Dramatic play is deliberately taking on the characteristics of another person and acting differently than themselves with the purpose of creating drama works. The main difference between creative and dramatic play is the intention. A student telling a doll what to do is imitating a parent in creative play, whereas in dramatic play a student becomes the parent so that they, and the audience, may learn what it is like to be a parent and to understand a parent's point of view.

CREATIVE PLAY
Children begin imitating the world around them at an early age. Playing with dolls mirrors what they see their parents doing with a younger sibling. Pretending to be a fireman or doctor helps them to understand the different roles people have in their lives.

When transitioning from creative play to dramatic play students learn the difference between their imaginary play and the real world.

DRAMATIC PLAY
There are many opinions on what dramatic play means. For the purpose of this book, it will refer to any form of drama which is created for a specific purpose and performed for an audience. Role playing, improvisation, skits, and plays are all examples of dramatic play.

ROLE PLAYING
Role playing involves creating short dramas, either scripted or improvised, that explore social issues in order to develop a better understanding of self, others, and various situations. It is a structured activity with a specific purpose intended. For example, an actor takes on the role of a new student so that they can have a better understanding of what that student is experiencing.

Some of the benefits for students participating in role playing are:
- it helps to develop compassion and understanding of another point of view;
- it provides an opportunity to express their side of a story or situation;
- it explores different methods for solving problems;
- it gives students the opportunity to experience different situations they may not come across such as bereavement or living in pioneer times;
- it develops acting, character development and writing skills.

Some suggested steps to teaching role playing are:
1. Develop rules of appropriate role play behaviour with your class at the beginning of the year. This can be included with your overall review of school and classroom policies. Even though sensitive subjects are being studied students still need to stay within the school rules.

Here are some rules you might like to establish with your class:
- don't make it personal;
- no swearing or inappropriate language;
- respect personal space.

2. Remind students that what is done during role play is not real and any negative comments about their character should not be taken personally. The key is everything said or done relates to the CHARACTER, not the ACTOR. Telling the big bad wolf in a role play that he needs anger management sessions is about the wolf, not the person portraying the wolf.
3. At first, be somewhat selective in who performs. The student who is being bullied in real life might not be strong enough to stand up in front of classmates to do a role play on bullying. Because a lot of role playing deals with sensitive themes, students need to separate the emotions they feel in real life from what the character feels. It takes a while for some students to be able to accomplish that.
4. Remind students that sometimes students, as actors, will need to say things, or behave in a way that goes against their personal beliefs during a role play. The purpose is to help them to develop understanding of what makes others behave the way they do and is not intended to change their personal point of view.
5. Role playing on its own can be used in any subject area. To make it part of your drama program drama skills need to be developed at the same time. This can be done by including in all role plays:
   - the creative process addressed in Chapter Two;
   - the elements of drama discussed in Chapter Three;
   - the elements of acting described in Chapter Twelve such as being aware of where the audience is, projection etc.

STEP IN, STEP OUT (ALSO KNOWN AS IN AND OUT)

A role-playing scene can either be acted from start to completion or using a technique such as step in, step out. This is a dramatic technique where the actor stops being their character in the middle of a performance so that they can discuss, as themselves, how their character is behaving and make connections to their own life.

Step in, step out can be useful for the following:
- Problem solving;
- Re-directing or bringing back to focus a script or improv that is getting heated or going on too long without resolution;
- Script development: What should happen next and why?
- Character development: What do you think your character should do next? Why? How do they feel about that?

Following is an example of step in, step out where the meaning of a scene is being explored.

Step in as an actress playing Red Riding Hood

Red Riding Hood: I think something looks odd about Granny. She has such big eyes and such a big nose.

Stop. Step out. (And now as yourself….)

> **Actress**: I'm not sure why Red Riding Hood can't tell it's a wolf. I would know if it weren't my real grandmother.
> **Another student:** Me neither. But maybe she doesn't see her Granny very often, and so she forgot what she looks like.
> **Actress:** Ah, that makes sense. Back then it probably took a long time to get to Granny's house. And maybe last time she visited she was too small to remember.

Step in. Continue in character.

Following is an example for using step in, step out to explore solutions to issues.

Step in as Giorgio who is being bullied in the playground.

> **Bully**: You give me your money, or I am going to tell everyone you stole it from me.
> **Giorgio:** But I need that money to get home on the bus.
> **Bully**: I don't care. Give it to me, or I'm going to slug you.

Stop. Step Out.

> **Actor playing Giorgio**: What could I do if I were in this situation? I could tell an adult. I could walk away.

Step in: (As characters...)

> **Giorgio:** I am going to go back to the classroom.
> **Bully:** Chicken baby. Go tell Mommy.
> **Giorgio:** I don't care. This is my money. (and walk away)

REAL VIOLENCE VERSUS FICTIONAL VIOLENCE

It is important to have a grade appropriate discussion about real violence versus fictional violence. Children today are constantly exposed to fictional violence through video games, cartoons, TV shows and movies to the point where they can't always distinguish between what is real and what are very clever special effects. Solutions to violent situations in real life don't resolve as neatly as they do in fiction. In a cartoon, a bully can be silenced by throwing a pie in their face. In real life that would not be advised. When using role play to come up with solutions to social issues those solutions need to be based on realistic options.

For an activity for exploring the difference between real and fictitious violence go to "Fact or Fiction" in Chapter Eighteen.

CHAPTER NINE
Helping Students Build Confidence when Performing

It would be unreasonable to expect students to be fearless when performing, nor is it necessary, but to develop creatively, students need to feel safe to express themselves without fear of negative feedback from their peers. Creating a supportive learning environment will encourage students to take creative risks, ease stage fright, and build self-confidence.

Some of the reasons students are not comfortable performing in front of their peers are because they:
- don't know how to step out of their comfort zones;
- fear that they will be laughed at;
- worry they will look silly;
- are anxious about assessment;
- suffer from stage fright.

These are all valid concerns which can be alleviated over time by implementing various strategies.

COMFORT ZONES
To develop performing skills, students need to go beyond what they are comfortable with. The challenge is helping students to expand their comfort zone without causing any negative repercussions. The goal is not to change someone but to help them see the potential in trying new things.

When it comes to performing there are three basic levels of comfort that most students will fall under.
1. No fear. There is always at least one ham or natural performer in each class who is the first to volunteer and appears to have no qualms about standing up in front of their peers.
2. Some fear. This is where the majority of the class will be. They won't be the first to volunteer but will need little coaxing to take a turn.
3. Too much fear. The remaining few will be the students who have a genuine fear of being the centre of attention.

There are many ways to help students stretch their comfort zone. Below are some strategies that can be used to help students become more confident performers.

- Brainstorm at the beginning of your drama year things that make people anxious about performing. Ask questions such as, "What makes you nervous?" or "What makes you reluctant to get up in front of your peers?" This will let students know they aren't the only nervous ones and that it is OK to feel that way.
- Let students know the performance expectations at the start of each lesson. Does everyone need to perform for this one? If no, tell them. The students who are chronically anxious can relax and focus on what is happening without the panic of "please don't pick me" running through their heads.

- Starting each drama lesson with five minutes of improvisation is a good way to get all students involved and used to performing. Use a bell for encouraging fearful actors. Let each student or group of students be on stage for 30 seconds then lightly tap the bell signaling their turn is over, and they can sit down. The 30 seconds will go by quickly leaving actors feeling that it wasn't so bad and proud of themselves for getting up.
- If students are given the choice to perform or not perform, then some will always choose the safe way and not perform. Give them the option at first, but the reality is that eventually you will need to see some work from them and the more they do it in small increments, the easier it will become for them.
- When possible, assign in advance the date and time students will be presenting dramatic works so that introverted students have the opportunity to prepare not just academically but also mentally.
- Have people perform in alphabetical order. Students will know when they will perform instead of anxiously wondering if they might be next.
- Start with groups. Performing in a group is less scary than performing solo and gives students the chance to get used to being in the spotlight without being the sole center of attention. There is courage in numbers.
- Give the time necessary for students to sufficiently practice before needing to perform. It is a lot more stressful if students are not prepared.
- Don't give critiques for the first few run-throughs of a new concept so that students can focus on the performance and not worry about what feedback or mark they will get.

FEAR OF BEING LAUGHED AT

Standing in front of a group of people to perform is not in a lot of people's comfort zones. And yet students are expected to stand up in front of their peers and perform on a regular basis not just in drama, but in all subject areas. Creating a safe learning environment so that students can develop their self-confidence and skills without fear of being laughed at or rejected is critical.

Following are some of the things a teacher can do in the classroom to create a learning environment that will encourage students to feel more confident performing in front of their peers.

- Establish rules of audience conduct at the beginning of the year.
- Establish rules for constructive feedback.
- Teach students the skills to feel confident.
- Step out of your own comfort zone and model how to do new drama concepts.

BEING A GOOD AUDIENCE

Students feeling comfortable performing in front of their peers begins with having a good audience. It is who they see when they get up to read a speech, answer a question, give a presentation, etc. Even the most self-confident presenter will quiver if met by a sea of unsupportive faces.

Learning how to be a good audience is not just important in drama. This spills over into all areas of school and life. For example, story time, reports, announcements, guest visitors, lessons, etc.

Rules of conduct are the behaviour that is expected from students while watching dramatic works. These rules should be reviewed at the start of the year and posted in the classroom. Some suggested rules are:

- Be a good listener. This means being an active listener by sitting still with hands to yourself, not talking when someone is talking and staying focused on the speaker.
- No laughing unless it is meant to be funny. Students often don't know the difference between laughing at someone and with someone. A good rule of thumb is if the laughter is hurtful or malicious then it's not funny. If someone slips on a banana by accident and hurts themselves, it is not funny. If someone slips on a banana on purpose and dramatically flails their arms while getting their balance it can be funny.
- Respond respectfully.
- Do not make inappropriate comments. These can be personal opinions such as "I am bored" or opinions not related to the story such as "Oooh, you like her" when the Prince proposes to the Princess.
- Show support. Clap even if you didn't like it. Look for positive things to say. Give constructive feedback that will help improve a performance or drama work.

Critiquing and analyzing

Critiquing and analyzing the work of others, as well as the student's own, is an important part of the creative process but can lead to reluctant performers if not delivered encouragingly. Brainstorm at the beginning of the year what is acceptable when providing feedback to peers. These can be used for any subject area where peer and self-assessment are used.

Some examples would be:
- Don't make feedback personal.
- Give positive feedback along with constructive ways to improve.
- Keep it relevant and directly related to what was just watched.
- Be sensitive to others and yourself by looking for the diplomatic way to point out areas that can be improved so as not to cause hurt feelings.

ASSESSMENT

Assessment is useful for helping students improve their work but can add to a student's anxiety when sharing their thoughts and ideas. At the start of the drama year, as students are developing their confidence in performing for their peers, hold off on assessing everything they do. If a student finally gets the courage to stand up and perform and then receives a C, they will feel discouraged and be reluctant to perform again.

STAGE FRIGHT

Being nervous before performing is normal, but if that fear is overwhelming, it can cause a person to be unable to perform. Certain things can help. These are as follows:

- **Acknowledge the fear**
  Telling someone they have nothing to worry about is saying their fear is not justified. Whatever the reason, it is real to that person.

- **Find the cause of the fear**
  If possible, find out what the person is scared of. In most cases it is a fear of messing up and looking bad in front of their peers. If the fear is stopping them from performing during a class assignment, try using some of the suggestions listed below. If the fear appears right before stepping on stage for the school musical remind the actor why they were chosen for their role and how important their character is to the plot.

- **Unhelpful underwear**
  The cliché response to nerves is to picture people in their underwear. Not only is this inappropriate to suggest to school-aged children but it is not very helpful and encourages actors to focus on something other than their performance. Following are some other techniques that may be helpful.

  - If you're giving a presentation eye contact is important. A confident performer can look the audience straight in the face, but most people will lose their focus. When speaking look just above the heads of the audience. It will seem like you're giving eye contact.

  - Look for a friendly face. You don't want to look at one person for the whole of a presentation but if you look for the people you know are there to support you, their encouraging smiles will help give you confidence.

  - Don't look at the audience. For a play, the characters you are communicating with are on stage. Unless your character talks to the audience or you're in a musical where you're often facing the audience, you shouldn't be looking anywhere but onstage.

  - Some people do well with something in their pockets such as a safety clip or stone to hold onto to help keep them calm.

BE PREPARED
This is the best way to help deal with stage fright. If someone hasn't been to practices or hasn't learned their lines, they will be more likely to make mistakes which in turn will make them more nervous. Confidence comes from being prepared. If an actor has been off book for half of the rehearsals, then even if they're nervous they will know their lines so well they will come out almost automatically.

PRACTICE MISTAKES
During drama classes and rehearsals develop strong improvisational skills so that if someone forgets their lines, they will know how to recover. Have a rehearsal where one of the actors deliberately forgets lines, misses their cues, etc. so that the other actors can improvise different strategies to keep the scene moving. This will help them know what to do when mistakes happen during a performance. Also, practice things like what to do if the power goes out during a media presentation, or the scenery falls down. Have a backup plan for anything that could go wrong

EXPAND OUTSIDE YOUR OWN COMFORT ZONE.
It can be difficult for teachers to model an acting skill if it is not in their own comfort zone. Some ideas to help performance-challenged teachers model lessons are:
- Have older student mentors come in at the start of a lesson to model the main idea.
- Invite a community professional, parent, or teacher expert to speak to the class.
- Have some of your more courageous students help you model the lesson.

CHAPTER TEN
Integrating Drama with the Rest of the Curriculum

Finding time to teach all the expectations for all subjects can be overwhelming, sometimes impossible. If you teach in a public school, you are required to cover all areas of the drama curriculum whether there is a spot assigned for it in the time table or not. Integrating the arts into other subject areas will help to accomplish this.

Following are some advantages to integrating drama.
- It provides the opportunity to cover several expectations in one lesson.
- It enables students to use their artistic interests to complement their learning in other areas which can lead to success and a better understanding of a subject.
- You can use drama as a means for students to demonstrate an understanding of all subjects when an academic expectation asks them to "describe" or "explain."
- When expectations in non-drama subjects state to use a variety of forms to communicate ideas, drama can be used as one of those forms.

It is still important to have dedicated time in the schedule for drama for the following reasons:
- The creative process and elements of drama need to be taught separately from the rest of the curriculum so that when students are asked to use drama works as a means to communicate ideas, they have the fundamentals in place.
- Students need to develop performing skills in a setting separate from other subjects so that the focus will be solely on acting.
- Having a designated time for drama lends importance to the subject.

INTEGRATING DRAMA WITH LITERACY
Integrating literacy with drama is a natural connection. A book and a play both tell a story. Both require the same creative process to create them, and both use dramatic techniques to read them out loud.

Below is a list of some of the ways drama and literacy can be combined.
- Re-tell a story as a play. Playwriting is a good way to practice the concepts of retelling a story. This can be done by taking out the descriptive language and deciding which dialogue is necessary to keep.
- Re-tell a play as a story. It's an interesting process to start with the dialogue of a play and turn it into a story by adding the descriptive components.
- Start each drama unit with a storybook that is relevant to the theme. For example, read "How to be a Friend" by Laurie and Marc Brown, to introduce a lesson on role playing to show acceptance.
- Borrow a concept from a book to create a drama work. For example, "No, David" by David Shannon, has a short sentence structure that lends itself to script writing. Chapter Eleven contains a lesson plan for this book.
- There are many opportunities for written assignments such as writing plays and skits, writing reviews for a play and keeping a drama journal.

Retelling a Story (Photo: Jackie Bennett)
Three Little Pigs

Following are components of the language curriculum that can be covered using drama:
- retell stories in the form of a play, readers theatre, and storytelling
- make personal connections
- reading, speaking and presenting
- communicate ideas in a clear and coherent manner with appropriate vocabulary
- identify and describe characters
- write or tell a story for specific audiences using the creative process point of view
- listen and respond appropriately
- identify and understand non-verbal cues
- identify and create media works using voice and body language to express meaning

Following is a list of other subject areas with ideas as to how drama can be incorporated.

Art
- learn about artists through skits, tableaux, and presentations
- create 3D works of art (puppets and masks)
- create scenery and sets using symbols and colour to create specific moods

Dance
- create dances based on a play read or observed
- use dance to create short drama works to show things students experience in their lives

Math
- create short skits showing mathematical problems
- perform short improvs to demonstrate months, temperature, and time
- write a script explaining the process of collecting and organizing data through a survey

Music
- develop vocal expression by using dynamics, pitch, tempo
- explore and use instruments and music to create particular moods in drama works

Physical Education and Health
- use improv and guided movement to learn about the stages of life and the five senses
- create commercials to teach healthy eating and healthy habits
- create safety announcements about personal safety and safety at home and school
- create skits to show how to get help for various situations
- role play to learn about respectful behaviour, responding appropriately to people, coping with challenges in their lives, peer pressure, and social skills.
- perform skits to learn about TV violence versus real violence

Science
- conduct interviews in a talk show format to learn about topics such as protecting endangered species, space exploration, and maintaining a healthy environment for living things
- perform skits to show safety procedures, methods for handling animals, and the use of protective sports equipment
- write and perform speeches about Canadians who have made contributions to the world

Short Skit (Photo: Sarah Stubbs)
The growth of a plant

Social Studies
- role play to learn about important relationships, rules, places and events in the lives of students
- organize a cultural day with skits and presentations
- create short skits showing the lives of people in early civilizations, medieval times, and early settlers
- stage a mock election with students playing the parts of politicians
- build stages used in Greek theatre and create drama works using that style of acting
- create an award ceremony for students portraying the achievements and contributions of Indigenous people

CHAPTER ELEVEN

Lesson Plans

This chapter contains some activities from Chapter Eighteen that are described in greater detail here in the form of lesson plans.

CELL PHONE DRAMA (GRADE 2-6)

Activity: Each student will write and perform a cell phone drama.

Model: Arrange with someone from outside of the classroom to phone you on your cell phone a few minutes into your lesson. Apologize to the students for forgetting to turn your phone off. Answer it, and immediately hang up but continue a conversation without the students knowing there is no one on the other end.

An example of your conversation would be:

Hello? Oh, Mom, I can't talk. I'm in the middle of a class. *(Pause while listening to the phone.)* I'll call you back. I can't... *(Pause)* What happened to the hamster? *(Pause)* How did it get in the toilet? *(Pause)*

Continue for two minutes maximum, and then end the conversation. Have fun with it and see how long you can convince students it is a real call.

Cell Phone Drama (Photo: Sarah Stubbs)
Phoning for a ride because the bus broke down

Lesson:
1. Students will write a script for a one-minute cell phone drama inspired by your call. This drama work should include the following:
    - Who has phoned them?
    - Where are they when they get the call?
    - What are they doing when they get the call?
    - How do they feel when they get the call?
2. Students will memorize and practice their cell phone drama using pretend phones.
3. Students will then perform them for the class. The drama work begins when the teacher says, "Ring, ring."
4. Complete the creative process by evaluating their own and other's works.

Materials: A cell phone for the teacher, toy cell phones or any small object the size of a phone for the students.

CHARACTER ON THE WALL (GRADE 1-6)

Part One: Student on the wall

This introduction to character analysis can be done at the beginning of the school year to help students learn about their classmates.

- Each student will draw a picture of their whole body or their head on a large piece of art paper.
- In point form, students will write details about themselves over the corresponding section of the drawing. For example, on the head you could write black hair and, on the feet, write favourite shoes- sneakers.
- On the sides of the paper list other characteristics they wish to share such as age, likes/ dislikes, hobbies, personality traits, etc.
- Colour or decorate and post around the classroom.

Character on the Wall
Student

Part Two: Character on the wall (Grade 3-6)
Students will apply the concepts used in the first activity to describe characters from fiction.

- Choose a story or a play that will be read or studied and make a list of the main characters.
- Using a piece of paper the length of a student, trace around a volunteer to create a life-size silhouette or have the student draw a life-size body.
- Make one for each of the main characters in the story and post them around the classroom or in the hall.
- Ask students to write on the corresponding paper everything they know about each of the characters.
- As the story or play is read details can be added to the drawing as students learn more about the character.

Character on the Wall—Fictional
Dorothy from the Wizard of Oz

Part Three: Character on the wall using the elements of drama (Grade 4-6)
Students will apply the concepts used in the second activity to extend their character sketches to include the elements of drama.

- Each student will choose a character from a story or play being studied and draw the outline of that person on a large piece of paper.
- They will fill in details relating to their chosen character, including the element of drama.

For example, if Julius Caesar is chosen, the following could be written on the character drawing:

Time: 100 BC to 45 BC
Place: Roman Republic
Character: tall, fair complexion, Roman ruler
Costumes: toga

Materials: Art paper and large paper roll

COMMERCIALS (GRADE 1-6)
Writing commercials can be done to show understanding of expectations from a particular subject or can be created to explore influence, purpose and audience of advertisement.

Following are some ideas for commercials that are curriculum related. Ask students to include vocabulary related to the subject when creating their drama works.

- Any object or service from history can be advertised such as a horse-drawn cart, the first wheel or blacksmith.
- Travel commercials can explore reasons to visit or move to a country or time in history. Dwellings, available jobs, and climate are some of the details that can be mentioned.
- Real estate commercials encouraging people to buy a house from now or in the past.
- Recruitment ads looking for people to move to a new location can be made. An example of this would be:
  Are you finished school or your apprenticeship? Upper Canada is looking for you. Own a piece of land. Live close to a community with blacksmiths, millers, shopkeepers. Put your education to work.

CREATING COMMERCIALS

1. Either alone, or in small groups students will choose or create a product that will be advertised.
2. The groups will write the commercial either as a script to perform or written in point form to perform as an improvisation.
3. Things to include are:
   - the product name
   - reasons to buy it
   - a demonstration on how to use it
   - the cost
   - where it can be purchased
   - a jingle and slogan.
4. Groups will present their commercial.

WHO IS THE AUDIENCE? (GRADE 4-6)

Commercials are written with a target market in mind. Writing scripts that adapt to different audiences is an important concept that can be used when creating drama works for other assignments.

1. Brainstorm how and why various audiences would respond differently or the same to something.
2. Each student will create commercials for a real or invented product for a specific audience, such as teenagers, and perform it for the class.
3. Write on separate flash cards different age groups such as child, teen, parent, and senior.
4. Students will present their commercial again, but this time they will adapt the delivery according to which flash card you hold up.
5. Discuss the changes that needed to occur to adapt to the various audiences.

Materials: Flashcards

MAKING TOAST (GRADE 4-5)

Sequencing in the correct order is important for writing drama works as well as when giving instructions for someone to follow.

1. Give each student an index card or small piece of paper.
2. Each student will write in point form the steps needed to make toast.

3. Collect them. Choose several of the cards that are missing key details and step by step follow the instructions exactly as written to make toast, making sure you don't automatically fill in some of the steps. For example, if a student writes butter your toast, don't use a knife, as it wasn't stated. Students will quickly learn the importance of making sure they include all the details. An example of the first run would be:

Read out loud the instructions from a student's card.
Student instruction: Put bread in a toaster.
The teacher would try to put a whole bag of bread in the toaster.

Read another set of instructions:
Student instruction: Take a piece of bread out of the bag.
The teacher would take a piece of bread out of the bag.
Student instruction: Put the bread in the toaster.
The teacher puts a slice of bread in the toaster.
Student instruction: Take it out and butter it.
Because it didn't say to use a knife, butter the bread with your finger.

4. After a few unsuccessful attempts to make toast, ask students to rewrite their instructions on the back of their card.
5. Select one that is complete and successfully make toast following their instructions.
6. In pairs, students will now write instructions on how to do an activity that can be done in the classroom such as tying their shoes. With their partners, they will follow the instructions and give feedback for changes.

Materials: A loaf of bread, toaster, extension cord if needed, margarine, plastic knife, paper plate, index cards.

NO DAVID (GRADE 1-3)

This lesson uses the format of a published book as inspiration to create a new drama work.
1. Read *No David* by David Shannon to the class. Discuss the writing style and the use of illustrations to tell the story.
2. In pairs, students will think of a situation where a child doesn't want to do something and make a list of what those things might be. For example, if the character is Danielle who doesn't want to go to school, she could hide under the bed, feed her breakfast to the dog or hide the car keys.
3. Using the situation and character they will create a short script using only two words, the character's name and no, and create a series of tableaux to illustrate the story. Additional words can be added at the end of the story if needed.
4. One person will read the story, and the other person will create the tableaux. At the end, the actor performing the tableaux will say one line to conclude the story.

Using the situation where Danielle doesn't want to go to school, the drama work could look like this:
Narrator: No, Danielle!
Tableau: Danielle is hiding under her covers.
Narrator: No, Danielle!

Tableau: Danielle is feeding her breakfast to the dog.
Narrator: No, Danielle!
Tableau: Danielle hides the car keys in the plant.
Narrator: No, Danielle!
Tableau: Danielle refuses to go through the school door.
Narrator: No, Danielle!
Tableau: Danielle is having fun in gym class.
Tableau: Her mother (the narrator who joins the tableau) is frustrated because Danielle won't put her coat on.
The actor: I love school. I want to stay.
Narrator: No, Danielle!

5. After all the students have performed, they will turn their drama work into a picture book with illustrations that match their tableaux. They will then read it to the class.

Materials: *No David* by David Shannon. If this book is not available choose a book with a simple repetitive style that can be adapted to a drama work using a narrator and tableau.

RUBRICS (GRADE 1-6)
Rubrics as a form of assessment are more effective if students know how they are created and how to interpret them.
1. Explain to the class what a rubric is.
2. Brainstorm what would make the perfect teddy bear and write down their suggestions
3. Choose the top four answers by either voting or go with the most common ones.

    Top 4 attributes could be: 1) is in good condition 2) has nice accessories 3) is cuddly 4) can sleep with it.

4. Then make a rubric. An example would be:

Level 1	Level 2	Level 3	Level 4
the bear is not in good condition with rips and stains	the bear has some dirt on it	the bear is in good condition	the bear is in brand new condition
bear isn't cuddly	the bear is a little bit cuddly	the bear is cuddly	the bear is cuddly and very soft
bear is totally plain	the bear has an accessory	the bear has 2 or 3 accessories	the bear has lots of accessories with changes of clothes
unsuitable to sleep with	could sleep with it but not ideal	good to sleep with	the only animal you want to sleep with

5. Show the class one teddy bear at a time that you have brought for this lesson. Stuffed animals should be in various sizes and conditions making sure one is not a bear, and one is a beautiful stuffed bear that doesn't meet the expectations due to something like it isn't cuddly or can't be slept with. Students will decide where the bear fits on the rubric.
6. Once students understand this concept, divide the class into small groups to create their own rubric for an item you assign.

   For example, they can make a rubric for decorated cookies.
   - Bring in undecorated cookies with various things to decorate them with.
   - Students will create a rubric assessing how a well decorated cookie should look.
   - They then decorate the cookies.
   - Within their groups, students will assess their creations using the rubric.
   - Cookies are eaten.

Curriculum related areas where students can make and use rubrics would be when making 3D shapes with toothpicks and marshmallows, artwork, structures, skits, paragraphs etc.

Materials: Five stuffed animals of various conditions, chart paper, materials for an additional activity such as decorating cookies.

SOUNDSCAPE (GRADE 1-6)

A soundscape is when a short story is created relying completely on sound effects. The most effective ones have a story that builds in the middle and returns to calm.

One of my favourites I learned at a leadership conference is "Making Rain" and is a quick one to teach students.

This is how to do it.

1. Students can sit in a group or remain at their seats. The more people that take part in this, the more impressive the rain will sound. Consider doing it for an assembly. There is no talking.
2. Someone is the leader. The first time through it should be the teacher or someone who is familiar with this activity.
3. The first step is for the leader to rub his hands together swiftly. Starting at one side of the room, the audience directly in front of the leader will begin to rub their hands together. They then slowly move from one side of the audience to the other. The rest of the audience mimics the leader when they receive eye contact and will continue the action until the leader returns with a new action.
4. When everyone is rubbing their hands together the leader goes back to where they started and will continue with the second step.
5. In step two, the leader starts clicking their fingers on both hands. The audience continues rubbing their hands until the leader gives them eye contact. They then start clicking their fingers. The leader continues across the group until everyone is now clicking their fingers. At each step there will be a point where there is a mix of the previous action and the current one.

6. The next step is slapping your hands on your knees. As before, people will go from clicking to slapping when the leader looks at them.
7. The fourth step is to start stomping on the floor with people going from slapping to stomping.
8. Continue this process in reverse. Slapping your knees, clicking your fingers, and then rubbing your hands.
6. When everyone is rubbing their hands again, the last step is the silence after the rain. The leader puts their finger to their lips. Everyone will stop rubbing their hands when the leader faces them until the room is silent.

Now that you've made rain break the students into smaller groups to create and present their own soundscapes. Sound effects can be made using their bodies, voices or objects found in the classroom.

Below are some ideas for creating soundscapes.
- Make a thunderstorm. Begin with silence, then thunder in the distance followed by rain falling, wind, etc. until the peak is reached. Then reverse the process as the thunder goes away in the distance and silence returns.
- Recreate a day from wake-up to bedtime. The alarm goes off, yawn, pour cereal into a bowl, brush teeth, run to school, pencils scratching, etc. until the end of the day when you go home and go to sleep.
- A canoe trip can have the sound of paddling down a peaceful river that moves into noisy rapids, approaching a waterfall, sound of a paddle furiously trying to steer the canoe away, the sound of people yelling, thud of canoe landing, more paddling, water gets slower until peaceful paddling again.
- A noisy classroom can begin with students working quietly. When the teacher leaves the room, the class will get increasingly noisy until the teacher comes back in, and students go back to quietly working.

POLITICAL SPEECHES (GRADE 5)
This lesson is geared towards students learning about the election process.
1. Divide the class into four to six groups representing fictitious political parties.
2. Students in each group will brainstorm what their party would like to achieve when they are principal for a day. (Ask the principal if they would be willing to let the winning party be principal for the day. If no, then students will base their platform on what they would do if they had the chance to be principal.)
3. Each person in the group will be assigned a different grade or audience to speak to. For example, one student might speak to a Grade 1 class, another will speak to the Grade 8 class, and another to the office staff. If one of the groups has fewer students in it, someone will need to speak to more than one group.
4. Each group will do the following:
    - choose a party name, slogan, and main platform;
    - make posters;
    - discuss different audiences and how they would need to adapt their speech to suit the age group;
    - will write a one-minute speech to explain why someone should vote for them while keeping in mind who their audience will be.

5. Students will adapt their party's platform to the audience they will speak to. For example, when speaking to a Grade 1 class, you might tell them you will provide longer recess. But if speaking to a parent group, you would focus on explaining you want to give their children more exercise by lengthening recess. Students can promise anything they want as long as they can explain how they will achieve this. Note: Someone needs to tell younger students that this is not real, and they will not be getting what is offered.
6. The teacher will ask other teachers or audiences if the student parties can come to their classrooms for ten minutes to give speeches followed by a vote. You will need the same number of audiences as there is the number of students in a group. For example, if the groups have five students in each one, you will need five different audiences to take part.
7. Dressed professionally, students will go to their audience to give their one-minute speech. After the speakers from all the parties are finished, hand out ballots for the audience to vote for which group they would like to see as principal for a day. Put the ballots in a separate envelope for each class riding.
8. When all the students return, tally the votes for each audience. Each riding will have a winner. The party who has the most location wins will be the winning party.
9. Each person will assess how they did individually and why they think the outcome was the way it was.
10. If the winning party actually gets to be principal for the day, book a date and have the party meet with the principal to discuss what will happen.

Materials: Poster materials

SILENT MOVIES (GRADE 4-6)

Because silent movies didn't have sound the facial expressions and gestures of the actors were important to convey the story. Therefore, creating silent movies is a good project for helping students develop those skills as well as providing an opportunity to work with technology.

1. Show an age-appropriate silent movie. These can be found on the internet.
2. Discuss the elements of silent movies and how they differ from modern movies. When having this discussion note that some of the old films have been revitalized with music added. When these movies were originally played in a theatre, the accompanied music was performed live by a piano player.
3. As a class, choose a story concept based on a subject being taught in Social Studies. For example, a snowstorm that occurs during school in pioneer times.
4. As a class write the script, or have small groups write the script and then use the class favourite. The script will be comprised of short sentences that will be filmed to tell the story in between the action. Use as many word panels as is necessary to tell the story concisely and believably. Aim for five to ten minutes maximum.
5. Decide what costumes will be worn.
6. Create a scenic backdrop from a large piece of paper that represents the overall theme of your story.
7. Make the script panels for your story. This either can be done as part of a computer movie program or printed off to be filmed. The panels will be placed between the filmed action.

8. Assign the roles played by the students either through auditions or volunteers. Practice with someone reading the title pages out loud.
9. Film the segments. There are three ways you can film depending on the editing capabilities of available movie programs:
    - it can be filmed out of sequence and edited later on the computer;
    - it can be filmed in sequence and the title pages later inserted using a movie program
    - it can be filmed in sequence stopping to film the title pages that you will have sticking on the wall so that no editing needs to be done at the end.
10. If you will be using the first two options for filming the segments load your movie clips on to a computer program that allows editing. If you have filmed out of order, place the scenes in the correct order and add the word panels if they weren't filmed. Depending on the capabilities of your students a teacher or volunteer may need to do this step.
11. Because there was no sound used in silent movies live piano music was used to accompany the film to create the mood while the movie was being shown to audiences. Brainstorm with the class what type of music will be needed for each of the sections. For example, if the word panel says, "I have terrible news to tell" you would have slow scary music or "Run for your life" would need music with a faster tempo. You will need someone who can play or record piano music.
12. Play the completed movie, with piano accompaniment, for the class to see and review it. If any significant issues need to be fixed, do so.
13. Invite parents and friends to come for a movie night or afternoon complete with beverages and popcorn. Because the movie is not very long consider combining it with another activity such as student-led conferencing or an arts evening.

Materials: Costumes, cue cards, video camera, large paper, movie editing software, piano or keyboard, piano player

CHAPTER TWELVE

Acting

Acting is not something that can be taught in one chapter or even in one book. Much of acting is based on practice, talent, and experience and can take years to develop. However, when teaching drama and directing plays, there are ways to help students to become stronger actors.

WHO ARE YOU SUPPOSED TO BE?
Acting at the primary/junior level usually comes under two categories: playing yourself and being someone you're not.

Playing Yourself
Playing yourself, even when you're playing a character, is when you use your own voice and mannerisms. In many classroom assignments, the emphasis is more on developing drama works. For example, the focus in a role play about bullies is about bullying prevention as opposed to developing the acting skills of the person playing the bully. Therefore, students will use their own voice and mannerisms even if the script is about someone else.

Being Someone You're Not
When the focus of a drama assignment is on acting, students will develop the skills necessary to act like someone other than themselves. Creating strong, believable characters that are different from the actor portraying them can be developed through research, observation, empathy, relating to personal experiences, and practice.

1. Research
By researching a character, actors can learn things that will help make a character more believable. For example, if you are in a historical drama such as *The Diary of Anne Frank*, what was it like during the war? How were Jewish people treated? What other stories about people needing to hide during a war could help you to understand Anne? Because she was a real person, is there documentation that shows character traits, clothing, living conditions, emotions she would have felt, etc.? Answers to all these questions help students gain a better understanding of the character and leads to a more believable performance. For fictitious characters, students can research similar non-fiction people to make connections.

2. Observation
Observing people who are similar to the character can help to make an actor's character more believable by imitating their accents, body language and personality traits.

3. Empathy
There will be fictitious characters that will be difficult to research and no real people to observe with similar characteristics. For example, few people will know a wolf who blows down houses. This is where empathy comes in. What would it feel like to be a wolf that no one likes or who always gets into trouble? Why is he so mean? Understanding what motivates a character can help make the portrayal more realistic.

4. Making personal connections
When actors are playing a character who does or feels things that they have not experienced themselves, they can look for personal life connections that are similar. They can draw on those experiences to develop characterization.

5. Practice
Acting involves using the whole body. To do this, an actor cannot truly become a character until their lines are well-memorized. Reading from a script or thinking about the next line will distract the actor from being able to develop the mannerisms and emotions needed to portray their character. The sooner actors are off-book, the more time they can spend at rehearsals developing a believable character.

ACTING STYLES
Acting styles are different depending on which drama form is being used. Following are some examples of how the actor needs to adapt their acting style depending on where they perform and what the theatre form is.
- In early Greek theatre where actors were at the bottom of a hill performing for a large audience, actors needed to use exaggerated gestures and wear large masks so people at the top of the hill could see them.
- Comedy and children's theatre often use exaggeration to make characters, particularly villains, funny.
- Film acting began with exaggerated facial expressions and body language because there wasn't any sound. Actors don't need to exaggerate their expressions and body language in contemporary movies because the camera is close up.
- Contemporary stage acting often has the benefit of microphones so actors sound more realistic without using booming voices that lose some of the realism in order for people in the back rows of the theatre to hear them.

BLOCKING
Blocking, the art of assigning where actors move during a play, is usually done by the director. Some directors like to block out every movement. Others will give the basic instructions and then let the actor move where and when they feel it is natural to do so. For in-class acting assignments, students will usually plan their own blocking.

These are some things for actors to consider when self-blocking.
- Why am I moving? Would my character do this?
- Don't just stand there. Find the balance between continually moving, which is distracting to the audience, to staying in one spot which can be boring for the viewers.
- What are you doing when someone else is talking? Are you listening intently or squirming in your seat? Whatever you choose to do, it must be done in character.

Some basic blocking rules to keep in mind when actors are onstage are:
- Don't stand between the person speaking and the audience.
- Don't stand with your back to the audience when you are speaking.
- Don't have your back to the audience unless necessary.
- Don't wander behind the site lines.
- Don't stand in a straight line with other actors unless there is a reason.

- When walking across the stage with someone, the shorter person is closest to the audience.

MISTAKES

The number one rule when an actor makes a mistake during the performance of any drama work is to fake it, and chances are no one in the audience will know a made a mistake has been made.

Ways to make a mistake obvious are:
- pause and hum and hah or even worse say something like, "Ohhh, I forgot my line"
- cry and run off stage
- ask someone for your line
- give someone their line
- stand there and say or do nothing while everyone stares at each other

Some hints for faking it are:
- Stay in character.
- Improvise a line or two to get things back on track, either for yourself or another actor.
- If no one seems to be able to move the story forward, then sometimes someone needs to say their next line even if it doesn't make much sense.
- Sometimes, something so wrong happens that no covering will make up for it, such as a door falling over. Ignore and continue is an option, but the door did fall over so the audience will be distracted by it. You can make a joke about it. If you're in the middle of a fairy tale, you can say something like, "I think the big bad wolf must be close by." Or if something like a lamp falls over, walk over while still saying your lines and pick it up, and continue.

Why do young actors forget lines?
- Sometimes they lose focus. They get distracted by something else like parents waving from the audience or camera flashes going off. Or they're tired and not paying attention.
- They don't know their lines well enough. The sooner actors are off-book, the better chance there is they will remember their lines. Also, by avoiding the use of a prompter, actors will have the opportunity to practice their improv skills.
- Stage fright can make an actor freeze up with no hope of a word coming out. Again, this is why knowing your lines well and having sufficient practice is essential. Stage fright will still exist, but when actors are used to performing in front of their peers on a daily basis in rehearsals, it won't be as scary on opening night. Giving your actors the skills to deal with any situation that may arise will go a long way to helping with their stage fright. It is harder to be afraid you will mess up if you know how to fix it when you do.

COMMON PERFORMANCE PROBLEMS

Following is a list of the common issues to be aware of that will distract the audience during a performance. These can all be addressed during rehearsals.
- The actor is not loud enough.
- The actor is upstaging another actor or showing off.
- The actor has their back to the audience.

- People forget their lines.
- One actor gives another actor their line.
- Students are seen peeking from the wings to watch the performance.
- Stage fright.
- Students talking or fooling around off stage.
- Actors talking on stage when their character is not speaking.
- Actors waving to their parents when onstage.

CHAPTER THIRTEEN

One-Act Plays

PERFORMING ONE-ACT PLAYS

One-act plays are an excellent way for students to work on acting skills without having to memorize a lot of lines, and they require fewer rehearsals than a full play. One-act plays can be any length, ranging from five minutes to an hour.

If students will be performing or writing one-act plays, this should be done towards the end of the year after there has been plenty of time to develop the necessary drama skills.

One-act plays can be used for the following:

1. Performing for the school or parents
- Have an evening of one-act plays. By having more than one play, more students will have the opportunity to play a starring role.
- Put on a one-act play before another production such as a short musical.
- Include one-act plays as part of the school's arts night.

2. Working on drama skills in the classroom
- Short plays help students develop drama skills such as character development, script analysis, and performance techniques.
- Because of the length of one-act plays, several can be used so that all students have the opportunity to take part.
- One script can be chosen with small groups all preparing the same play. This will provide the opportunity to compare acting styles and interpretations.

Where to Find Scripts
- Use one that is already published. There are various books and magazines with collections of plays available at the library or to purchase. If you search on the internet, many sites pop up for free one-act plays for children.
- Some one-act plays have been included at the end of this book that may be used with permission for classroom learning.
- Teachers can write a play. You know your students, what issues they may have experienced or what they are interested in. You also can write a play where you create enough characters for all your students to take part.
- For grades four and higher, students can write their own play. This will not only develop playwriting skills but will allow them the opportunity to use the creative process and elements of drama as part of one assignment.

Writing One-Act Plays
Before beginning to write a play there are some differences between writing a play and writing a story to keep in mind.

Script
- A play traditionally has the character name and dialogue written in the centre of the page or can sometimes be at the lefthand side of the page with their spoken words beside it.

An example of a script that is centred:

Pippa
When is lunch?

Mama
You just had lunch.

Pippa
I meant breakfast.

Mama
You had breakfast before you ate lunch.

An example of a script that is formatted from the left:

Pippa When is lunch?

Mama You just had lunch.

Pippa I meant breakfast.

Mama You had breakfast before you ate lunch.

- There are no dialogue descriptions such as, 'Pippa said with her stomach rumbling' in a play.
- Other than at the beginning of a scene there are no descriptions of location, colours or style of furnishings.
- A script only tells you who is speaking and what they are saying. On occasion, the playwright will add notes to help with the interpretation.

Scene Changes
In a book, the story can jump from scene to scene effortlessly. On stage, it is not so easy. Limiting the number of scene changes will make the production easier to mount.

The same goes for time. If the play shows the ageing of a character over a few years or keeps switching back and forth between years, this will be hard to portray without taking lots of breaks to adjust makeup and costumes.

Writing a One-Act Play Using the Creative Process
Using the five stages of the creative process is particularly important when developing plays.

1. Developing creative ideas
Developing a play begins with an idea of what the story will be about. This may be an idea that is already in mind or comes from a list resulting from brainstorming.

2. Planning
Once the main idea has been chosen planning begins. The following questions need to be answered:
- What is the main idea or theme?

- What characters are needed?
- Where does the story take place?
- What year and time is it?
- Who is the audience?
- Where will it be performed?
- How long should it be?
- What is the beginning, middle and end?
- What form will it be? Comedy? Puppet show?

The next step is to create the script. Begin with an outline of the story, either in point form or using a storyboard to show each scene. Then the script will be written and edited until a satisfactory working copy has been produced.

3. Practicing
Rehearse the scenes with actors reading the parts to see if the play works when it is read out loud. Revise and edit the things that need to be changed to make a strong final draft.

4. Performing or sharing your work
Invite the intended audience to attend a production of the play.

5. Analyzing and reflecting
After the performance evaluate how the play went based on the production and audience feedback. Reflect on what went well, what could be improved, and what was learned from the process of creating the play. If needed, make any changes to make the script stronger.

Writing a one-act play using the five elements of drama
When creating a play, the elements of drama need to be considered.

1. Character

Number of characters
Use only the characters that are necessary in a scene. Avoid characters that have one line or are only in one scene. Too many characters mean more actors are needed than you might have.

Character development
Lines need to show the audience who the character is, either by what they say about themselves or by what others say about them.

Character Types
Each play needs the following:
Protagonist: the main character
Antagonist: the character who conflicts with the main character
Supporting Actors: smaller parts to help tell the story

2. Relationship
What is the relationship between the characters? How do they relate to each other?

Do they hate each other? Do they know that the other person hates them? How does this affect what they say or do? These are some of the many questions that can be asked when developing characters.

3. Time and Place
Where does the story take place? What time of day is it? Does the play take place over one day or span over several days? What year does it take place?

4. Tension
The play needs to lead somewhere. What is the climax, or the critical point in the play? Is there a problem to be solved? How will the story get there? After the climax of the play, there should be just enough dialogue to wrap the story up.

5. Focus and Emphasis
What is the main purpose or idea of your play? Is it about bullying? Surviving a birthday party? Solving the theft of coleslaw?

Why plays should be performed
When students create longer dramatic works, there isn't always time available for them to be performed, especially if students have each written a play. There are, however, several significant benefits to having a play performed after it has been written. These benefits are:
- it provides playwriters the opportunity to see what works and needs to be improved;
- it makes the characters come alive and change depending on the actor playing the part;
- it completes the playwriting process as plays are written to be performed;
- it provides valuable audience feedback.

CHAPTER FOURTEEN
Drama Games

This chapter has a collection of quick games that can help develop drama skills as well as be used as icebreakers at the beginning of a school year or a production. Games are useful if you have time to be filled or need a transitional activity between subjects.

Note: Many of these games are not ones that I have created. They are a collection of games I have seen played or have played myself over the years.

AIR SPORTS (GRADE 1- 6)
Purpose: developing focus and concentration

Students will pretend to play various sports without props using the appropriate number of players. For example, tennis would need two to four students. The key is to watch the other people playing so that you can respond with the appropriate aim and timing.

ALL THOSE STUDENTS WHO (GRADE K-2)
Purpose: learning to categorize while learning about each other

Call out to the class different things that categorize students and give them an action to go with it.

An example of this would begin with the teacher saying: "All those students who had waffles for breakfast jump up and down." Students who had waffles will jump up and down while the rest of the class remain seated. Then the teacher could say, "All those students who made their bed act like monkeys." Students who had waffles for breakfast and made their bed remain standing while they act like monkeys. Students who had waffles but didn't make their bed will sit down. Continue until the time is up.

Try to vary the characteristics so that some will have all students participating such as "all those people wearing socks today wiggle your nose" to more obscure commands such as "all those students who have been to Spain wave hello."

CAST A SPELL (GRADE: 1-3)
Purpose: staying in character

The teacher, or a volunteer, will cast a spell on the class that will dictate how they will behave for a set time. For example, if the leader says, "Everyone is a skater" students will move around the room as a skater until the spell is removed. The spell can last as long as you want, even while regular learning continues.

CHARACTER ON MY BACK (GRADE 3-4)
Purpose: to use leading questions

This popular party game helps students learn to ask effective questions to discover their identity. Each student will have the name of a character taped to their back. They will ask another student a question about their character that requires a yes or no answer in hopes of guessing who they are. For example, "Did I invent something?" or "Am I a fictional character?"

Students have one guess after each question. If they guess correctly, they sit down. Continue until all characters have been guessed or time is up.

CHARACTER TRAITS (GRADE 4-6)
Purpose: developing improvisational skills and character analysis

On individual pieces of paper write the names of characters from familiar books. Each student will draw out one name. Thinking about the traits that character has, the student will perform an improv without using their character's name. The other students will guess who they are. When someone guesses correctly the student will sit down after choosing the next person to act out a character.

CRAZY SPORTS BROADCASTING (GRADE 4-6)
Purpose: developing creativity

Two or three students will play the parts of sports broadcasters who are reporting on a crazy sports event. They will pick a sport that is made up but report on it as if it was a real game, giving a play by play account.

The reporters will give a play by play account of a live crazy sports event while the actors playing the athletes do exactly what is being described.

Some examples of crazy sports would be speed typing, breath holding, no blinking, pizza throw, synchronized teeth brushing, etc.

Crazy Sports Broadcasting (Photo: Jackie Bennett)
No blinking tournament

DO YOU HEAR WHAT I HEAR? (GRADE 1-3)
Purpose: learning to be aware of one's surroundings

The group will remain silent for one-minute listening to their surroundings. When the minute is up, each student will write down everything they heard. Compare with the rest of the group. Points are given for each sound written down. Bonus points are given for a sound that no one else identified.

EMOTIONAL MIX UP (GRADE 1-3)
Purpose: learning about appropriate emotional responses.

Make two piles of cue cards with one pile representing various emotions and the other pile with events such as singing a solo, blowing out candles on a cake, changing a diaper, or scoring a winning goal. A student will draw a piece of paper from each pile and do a short improv based on the combination. For example, card one might say angry and card two changing a diaper.

HOT AND COLD (GRADE 1-3)
Purpose: learning about opposites

In pairs, students will pick two descriptions that are opposites that they will demonstrate to the class without words. Acting out one each, they will perform them simultaneously for their classmates to guess. Example: fast and slow, tall and short, or sad and happy.

PHOTO OP (GRADE 1-6)
Purpose: creating scenes

Ask someone to suggest a situation where a photo would be taken. Brainstorm things that make a photo interesting or funny such as someone sticking out their tongue or a child pulling someone's beard.

Divide the class into small groups. One group at a time will come to the front of the class. Give them a type of photo opportunity and twenty seconds to get into a pose for that photo. Each person should try to be a different character.

If you have a class camera assign a photographer to take an actual photo for people to see later.

Types of photo ops would be a family portrait, Santa at the mall, wedding, class photo, etc.

Emotional Mixup (Photo: Sarah Stubbs)
Emotion: Angry
Activity: Eating ice cream

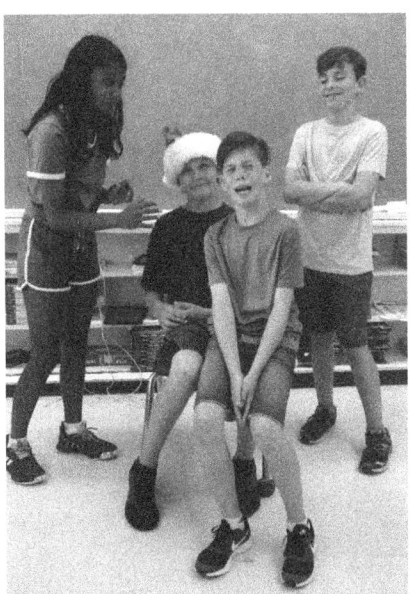

Photo Op (Photo: Jackie Bennett)
Photograph with Santa

PICTURE YOURSELF (GRADE 4-6)
Purpose: developing creativity

Bring to class a collection of pictures from magazines, newspapers, or personal albums. Individually or in small groups actors will choose a picture and recreate it as a tableau for ten seconds. Then they will step away from the tableau to improvise a scene based on what they think is happening in the picture.

POTLUCK (GRADE 1-6)
Purpose: getting to know people

Standing in a circle, students will take turns saying their first name followed by what food they could bring to a potluck lunch that starts with the same letter as their name. For example, "My name is Jackie and I am going to bring jam sandwiches to the potluck."

If someone can't think of food that starts with their initial, they will say, "My name is Jackie and I am going to help at the potluck." They will then sit down at their seat. Once everyone in the circle has had a turn repeat with the students still standing. They will now add another food item or sit down if they can't think of one. For example, "My name is Jackie and I am going to bring jam sandwiches and juice." Keep going until there is only one person left who will say, "My name is Jackie and I can't wait for the potluck."

You can play this with other categories such as animals or favourite words.

SPEECH BUBBLES (GRADE 4-6)
Purpose: developing creativity

Draw several large speech bubbles in a row on the blackboard. Students in small groups will create a short comic strip. Each person will be one of the characters in the comic. They will write their words in the bubble and then freeze in front of the bubble with an appropriate pose. The rest of the class will read the comic strip.

Take pictures of each comic and make a class comic strip book.

Speech Bubbles

STAND/BEND/SIT (GRADE 4-6)
Purpose: developing focus

Either using a script or improvising, students will act out a scene.

As they perform, only one actor can be sitting, standing, or be halfway between sitting and standing. As an actor changes positions in the scene, the others must also change to ensure only one person is doing each position at a time.

For example, if actor A is standing and actor B suddenly stands up, actor A must change position so they are not standing as well.

TAKE OVER (GRADE 1-6)
Purpose: developing improvisational skills

A small group of students will start an improvised scene. At any point the teacher will call freeze. The students performing will freeze and the teacher will select one or more students to take the place of the actors, who will take over in the exact position as the person they replace.

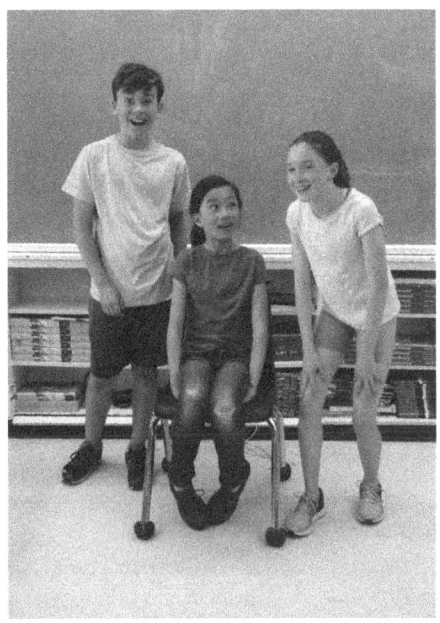
Stand/ Bend/ Sit (Photo: Jackie Bennett)

They will continue with the improvisation either with the same story or change it to a new story.

An example would be:

A person freezes in the middle of swinging a pretend tennis racket during a game. The new actor takes his place and continues trying to ward off giant mosquitos with the tennis racket which is now a fly swatter.

TEN SECOND OBJECTS (GRADE 1-6)
Purpose: using bodies to create objects

Students in small groups will have ten seconds to create an object using their bodies. All students in the group must be part of the object. State the object and then count down from ten. When you get to zero the students should be in the form of that object.

Examples could be a playground, a washing machine or a fruit salad.

TWO FACTS, ONE FICTION (GRADE 1-6)
Purpose: getting to know each other

A person will tell the class two things that are true and one thing that is false about themselves. The class will guess which is fiction.

An example would be:
Two truths and one lie about me is I've been ice fishing, I was in the opening ceremonies for the Skydome and I was born in Texas

WORD TENNIS (GRADE 1-3)
Purpose: learning to categorize

Divide the class into two rows facing each other. State a category, such as animals. A person on one side will say the name of an animal and then throw a spongy ball to the person opposite them. When that person catches the ball, they will say a different animal and throw the ball back to the person standing beside the person who last threw the ball. If a person can't think of an animal or they repeat one already said they would sit down. Continue until one side is all seated. The remaining row wins.

This is called word tennis because the ball goes back and forth like a game of tennis. Therefore, there should be a steady beat to the throwing and catching of the ball. If someone is taking too long to say a word they are out. Try having a student bang a slow, steady beat on a drum. If the game is going on too long speed up the drum beat so students need to think of answers faster.

CHAPTER FIFTEEN
Putting on a Play

This chapter will help you put on a play that students and parents will rave about and leave everyone satisfied. "Was it really an hour?" will become, "Is it over already?"

Why put on a play?
School productions are one of the few creative events where a large number of students with various levels of abilities can participate at the same time. Plays also provide an opportunity for students to use the drama skills practiced in class. Plays are a lot of work but with organization they can run smoothly and be very rewarding.

CHOOSING A PLAY
Firstly, a play must be chosen. Deciding who will participate in it will help to decide what form of play would be best.

Who will be in it?
Will it be the whole school, one of the divisions, or only those interested in taking part in the production?

- Whole School Production
  If the play is an annual event where everyone in the school from Grade 1 to 8 can try out, then a musical is the best choice. Musicals have more characters and have a chorus where an unlimited number of actors can be used.

  A note on whole school productions:
  It is more challenging to have a production where the age range of participants is from five to thirteen. You will run into supervision problems as your younger actors will not have the same attention span as the older ones.

- Divisional Production
  Even if only one division is taking part, there will still be too many actors to put on a play, making a musical more practical. Divisional productions are less stressful because the age range is easier to manage. However, with divisional plays, it usually means only one division can be involved each year which is disappointing to budding actors in other grades.

  When putting on a divisional play there are three options for casting.
  1. Use everyone in the division whether they audition for a part or not.
  2. Everyone who auditions will be part of the production.
  3. Only the actors needed are cast from those who auditioned.

- Only Those Interested
  If there is only a small group of students interested in putting on a production, you have the option of doing either a play or a musical. The cast can be selected from the whole school or within one of the divisions.

Overall, musicals are the best option because you can use a large number of students and you can use a broader range of talents such as dancers, singers, and musicians.

What play will you choose?

Once you have decided who will be taking part in the production, you need to choose a script. Several companies specialize in school plays; some are listed at the end of this chapter. You can order scripts online, or some music stores have a selection of musicals onsite. If possible, read potential plays before purchasing them to confirm they are appropriate for your school and that the story is something your actors and audience will enjoy.

Things to consider when choosing a play are:

Age appropriate
Is the story suitable for the performing age group? Is it a long script with a lot of lines to memorize? This would be better suited for older actors. Are there solos? Very few primary students have experience singing by themselves.

Budget
How much money is there to spend on the production? Plays and musicals all have a copyright performance fee. The shorter or lesser known the play, the cheaper it will be. Popular musicals such as *Peter Pan* and *The Wizard of Oz* are more expensive. Other expenses such as the set, costumes, and microphones should also be taken into consideration when choosing your play. If you sell tickets, you may get back some of your money, but you can't rely on that. Finding out how much money you have before choosing the play will determine your script options.

Accompaniment
If you are doing a musical, you need to consider where the accompaniment will come from when choosing a script. Some musicals come with CDs with instrumental tracks to use for the performance. Some musicals only come with sheet music. If this is the case, do you have someone who can play the piano well enough to accompany the singers?

Skills needed
Some of the characters may need specific talents for the actor to portray them. If there are a lot of solos, do you have strong singers auditioning? If one of the characters is a circus performer do you have a juggler in the school?

Set
Where does the play take place? If it takes part in ancient Rome, do you have volunteers and the money to build a Colosseum set and dress everyone in togas? If no, choose something that takes place in current time or requires a simple set.

How long should it be?
For an intermediate production two forty-minute acts with an intermission is appropriate. A junior play should be an hour at the most, with the primary show being around thirty minutes. If you want something longer for the parents to attend you can combine another activity with the performance such as an art exhibit, a short concert, or storytelling.

Do you have enough actors?
In general, most musicals written for the elementary school level have lots of characters so that more students can take part. If there are twenty parts, make sure you will have enough actors to fill the roles.

Where will the performance be?
If your stage area is small, then doing a large production may not be possible. Choose a play that fits your space.

School policies and philosophy
It is a good idea to run any choices by the head of your school. They may only want curriculum-based plays. They may not want scripts with characters or subject content that go against the beliefs of the school.

After considering all of the above and you have chosen your play, it is time to find actors to fill the roles.

AUDITIONS
An audition is where an actor demonstrates their acting abilities to help the director assign roles. Traditional auditions require the actor to prepare a short, memorized monologue related to the part they are trying out for. In the case of a musical, actors also need to prepare a vocal solo and a dance routine. It is not necessary to do any of this with primary and junior students, especially when most of them won't be asking for a particular role.

Several weeks beforehand, announce when and where the audition will be and explain what preparation, if any, is needed. Post a signup sheet for interested students.

At the auditions, before beginning, ask each student to fill out an audition form. A sample one is at the end of the chapter. After forms have been completed, give a summary of the plot and then explain the following to the whole group:
- What the audition procedure will be.
- Tell them that you will not applaud or make any comment other than to say thank you at the end.
- Let them know what to do at the end of their audition. For example, go out to recess or sit at the back of the room.
- If it is a public audition remind the students to be respectful while watching others perform.

Public versus private auditions
You have the choice of holding auditions with everyone present or having actors audition one at a time without an audience.

The advantages of having a public audition are:
- Supervision is easier. If you have thirty students show up for an audition and you're the only adult, it is better to have all the students stay in the audition room with you instead of being in the hallway unsupervised waiting for their turn.
- It gives you an indication of how well someone performs when there is an audience.
- If you have experienced performers at the audition, they can go first to give inexperienced students the opportunity to observe what is expected of them.

The advantages of a private audition are:
- Students who are too scared to perform in front of their peers may feel more comfortable performing in private.
- If students don't know what other students were asked to do for their auditions, there will be fewer questions from students wanting to know why they weren't asked to do the same things at theirs.
- There will be fewer hard feelings with students thinking they did better than someone who got a main part if they didn't see their audition.

Some suggestions on what students can be asked to do for an audition:

Prepared Monologues
In general, prepared monologues, where an actor comes to an audition with a memorized speech from a play, are better suited for intermediate or secondary students. If you wish to use them, you will find that most primary/ junior scripts do not have any substantial monologues to choose from. You will, therefore, need to provide one that is either from another play or one you have written yourself.

Cold Read
This is when the actor reads something he has never seen before. This is not an effective process for primary/junior readers and again is better suited for intermediate and secondary students.

Play Reads
Have the student read a section from the play they have practiced in advance.

Musicals
Ask the student to sing a short song a cappella if they want a part with a solo. If they're going to be in the chorus, it's not necessary to hear them sing unless there is a limit to the number of people you are casting. Any song they sing is fine, even a nursery rhyme so that you can hear the following:
- if they can sing in tune;
- the volume of their voice;
- what their vocal range is; and
- what the quality of their voice is.

Guided Audition
This involves the student reciting a nursery rhyme while being asked to change the delivery based on cue cards that are held up. This is a quick and easy audition exercise that is well suited for primary and junior students. Refer to audition improvs in Chapter Eighteen for more details on how to do this.

Why guided auditions work for primary and junior students:
- It's quick. Each person performs for a minute at the most. If they do well and you are considering using them for a speaking part in a musical, ask them to sing. Otherwise, they are free to go.
- There is no preparation for the actor.
- It gives you the opportunity to see their acting ability.

- It is not as intimidating for the students as traditional auditions. They are usually so busy looking to see what word is coming up next that they forget to be nervous.
- It's fun and entertains the students who are waiting for their turn to audition.

Where to hold auditions
If possible, hold the auditions in the space you will be performing the play in. Otherwise, choose an area that will accommodate a large number of students with minimal things they can get into while you are focused on the actors.

What to look for during the auditions:

Volume
Depending on your budget you might not have microphones at the performance so how loud the actor can speak will be important. If you can't hear someone speaking at their audition, you won't likely be able to hear them on stage without a microphone.

Focus
Are the students focused during their audition? If they are easily distracted by the audience or misbehaving, they may not be suited for a lead role.

Can they sing in key?
This is important for trying out for parts with solos but not as important if they will be in the chorus.

Expression
Does the person show the ability to portray a range of emotions with more than one vocal or facial expression?

Role
Where do you see them fitting into the play? Is there a particular part they seem suited for?

Use the audition form to keep track of your observations.

CASTING
Assign roles to the students you feel are best suited to play the part.
If there are not enough parts for the number of students you want to use you can:
- make up some parts using available talents. For example, if you have a student who plays the trumpet, make him a court herald who plays every time the king enters.
- extend some of the scenes where appropriate. For example, if you have some students who like to tell jokes or are magicians, have them entertain the audience between scene changes, or add a dance sequence to celebrate a wedding.
- share roles. For example, if there is a narrator, have two students take turns narrating.
- have 'extras', or non-speaking parts, like they do in movies. This can help make the scenes more believable. For example, in a medieval court scene

when the King is talking there could be someone holding a royal flag, guards beside him, servants waiting etc.
- divide the musical chorus into smaller groups. This can look like this:

Chorus A would consist of a small group of strong singers who can sing one of the chorus numbers on stage by themselves.
Chorus B could be a dance chorus with a group of students who dance on stage while the chorus sings.
Chorus C is the main chorus. All remaining people without parts would sit on bleachers at the two sides of the stage or on the auditorium floor for the whole performance and stand when they are to sing.

If you don't have enough actors for the parts you can:
- combine two smaller parts;
- have one strong actor play two parts if those characters are never on stage at the same time;
- have a backstage helper come onstage to be a character that only has a few lines.

Before final casting

Before casting any parts that might be challenging or embarrassing for a student, such as a boy dressing like a girl in one of Shakespeare's plays, it would be wise to confirm if the actor is comfortable playing the part.

Check with homeroom teachers before casting the main characters as they know their students better than you might. Do they have behavioural or attendance issues? Do they have a learning disability that will prevent them from memorizing large amounts of lines? Although this is all useful information to know, it shouldn't be your sole influence. Some of the best performers are those who have personal challenges. If someone is perfect for the part, then cast them with the knowledge that you will need a different approach during rehearsals when working with them.

Also, beware of the teacher who thinks their student is the best actor in the school and is putting the pressure on you to cast them. Sometimes students do better in their classroom than on a stage. And sometimes a person, no matter how talented they are, is not suitable for the part.

Cast List

Once you have chosen your actors, make a cast list to post in a prominent place. Not only will this let people know who was selected and what their role is, it also lends importance to the event.

REHEARSALS

Some things to decide before beginning rehearsals are:
- How many will you have?

This depends on the length of your play, the experience of the actors, and how many times a week you wish to practice. Some sources say you need a rehearsal per page of a script. For primary and junior productions twice a week for three months is usually sufficient. You can always cut back on rehearsals if things are going well, but if they're not, you will be glad you started early. If you hold auditions at the end of a term, actors can study their lines over the holiday. This will save time at the first

few rehearsals where students may stumble over unfamiliar words.
- How long should rehearsals be?

This depends on the age group. For primary students you should aim for approximately thirty to sixty minutes, junior sixty to ninety minutes, and intermediate up to two hours. Anything less than fifteen minutes isn't going to achieve anything unless you are working one on one with an actor or practicing solos. Lunchtime rehearsals are suitable for scene work, but once you start doing complete run-throughs, you will need to meet after school.

- Who needs to be there?

Not everyone needs to be at all rehearsals. Main characters will need more rehearsals, whereas the character with two lines only needs to come occasionally. At first, you don't need to practice scenes in sequence. This will help you to avoid having students come for rehearsals where they are only briefly needed or not needed at all.

For students waiting to practice their part, they can watch quietly, do their homework, or you can give them scenes from other plays to quietly act out that will help develop their acting skills.

Types of Rehearsals
- Read Through

The first rehearsal is the read through where the play is read out loud by the actors playing the parts. This is for the full cast so that they can see who is playing what part, hear the complete story, sing along with musical numbers, hear the overall vision of the director, and learn what is expected of them over the next few months.

- Scene Rehearsals

Not all scenes need to be rehearsed each time nor do they need to be in the correct order. Pick a time, day, and place you will meet each week and stick to it. Post a rehearsal schedule so that cast know when they are expected to attend and what scenes they will be practicing. If you have after-school rehearsals, send home a copy of the rehearsal schedule for parents with a tear-off portion for them to send back indicating they know when their child should be there. Make sure all scenes are rehearsed before moving on to full rehearsals. Scenes that aren't working well should be practiced more than others.

During the scene rehearsals you will:
- run through scenes;
- tell actors where and when they will enter;
- tell actors where and when they move on stage;
- have the cast work with their props and set pieces;
- stop and start the action when you need to give directions on things such as how to say a line or respond to other characters;
- help actors interpret their lines;
- encourage actors to speak louder if necessary;
- answer questions;
- learn songs and choreography if any.

Full Rehearsals

When you are about three weeks from the dress rehearsal, start having full play practices so that students get used to when their cues and entrances are. All props and set pieces should be used. Do not stop the performance to give notes unless necessary. Take notes and deliver them at the end of the rehearsal. The backstage crew and sound technicians should attend these rehearsals and do everything they will be doing during the performance.

During rehearsals, students should exit the stage where directed and then come back into the gymnasium or theatre through a side door and sit quietly to watch the play until it is time to go backstage for their next entrance. Discourage the cast from jumping off the stage to join the audience instead of exiting correctly.

Curtain calls, where actors come on stage at the end of a performance to take their bows, need to be practiced at the full rehearsals as well. Generally, the smaller parts come on first followed by the larger parts. The number of people in a group should not be larger than there is room for them to stand in a row across the stage.

Following is a suggested order of appearance for curtain calls:

1st row: the main chorus
If your chorus has been sitting on bleachers on the auditorium floor, they can stand where they are, hold hands, and bow. Otherwise, they come onto the stage in a line, hold hands, bow, and step backwards to make room for the next group entering.

2nd row: dance chorus and small singing chorus

3rd row: actors with smaller and medium parts

4th row: main characters

5th row: backstage crew, sound tech, and music director

They come out to bow and then move off to the side so that the fourth row can step back to the front.

Next, everyone gestures towards the director, who takes a bow, and then all the actors take one final bow. Finally, either the curtains will close or if there aren't any curtains, the cast leaves the stage row by row as the house lights come on.

Tech Rehearsal

A tech rehearsal is a complete run-through of the play where the main focus is on the technical aspects of the play such as lighting, sound, and set changes. This run-through is with the full cast in full costume to make sure that things such as the lights are focused in the correct spot and microphones are used correctly. In most elementary productions where there are not a lot of tech requirements, this can be combined with the dress rehearsal. Otherwise, schedule a tech rehearsal before the dress rehearsal. Run the play from the beginning but stop when something is not right technically.

Dress Rehearsal

A dress rehearsal is where the cast wears their full costumes and makeup for a run-through of the play. Actors are backstage or in their waiting rooms as if it were the real show. Have the first one a week before the performance date. This gives you enough time to find costumes for those cast members who didn't find one. Unless a character needs unique makeup, only costumes are required at this practice. You will need volunteers to help with supervising the students waiting in classrooms or the hall for their entrances. It is a good idea to have the same volunteers that you will have at the performance, so they are familiar with all entrances.

A day or two before the performance have a second dress rehearsal. You might consider doing this for the school. This will give the actors a chance to practice with a live audience. At this rehearsal, run it without stopping as if it were a real performance with full costumes, makeup, set, lighting, and sound. Any issues can be ironed out after the rehearsal.

THE PERFORMANCE

Everyone has been working hard for countless hours over the past few months. Now you're ready to open the curtains. Have one last check before the performance begins to make sure:

- all props, sets, sound system equipment and costumes are in good condition and in their proper places. Have extra batteries on hand for microphones in case they die during a performance.
- all the actors have arrived. An attendance list is important for all rehearsals so that you can keep an eye on anyone who is missing too many but is also critical for the performance because it is easy to miss someone in all the excitement. Having cast members arrive an hour before the performance gives you a chance to locate the students who will swear they thought the play was next week. Communication to parents along the way is essential.

Nerves, nerves, and more nerves!

It is understandable that your young actors will be nervous, and this will be demonstrated in various ways from the child running up and down the halls like a wild thing to the child who is weeping hysterically in the bathroom refusing to come out. Each child will react differently and should be dealt with accordingly. Overall it will be essential to keep everyone quiet and calm. Ask the cast to bring a quiet activity that will keep them occupied while waiting for their turn to go on stage. Students should not leave their waiting rooms until it is their cue, or if a bathroom break is needed.

POST SHOW

There are only a few things left to do. These are as follows:

- Leave the performance area and waiting rooms tidy with all personal belongings taken home.
- Return props to where they came from. If you bought them, decide where to store them, or give them away.
- Take down the scenery and set and either store it or donate it.
- Thank all the cast and volunteers with a personal thank you by email or with a card. You may also wish to do this during morning announcements the day after the performance.
- Have a cast party to celebrate the end of the play. This is a fun way for actors to talk about their memories and spend time relaxing after all their hard work.

It is not usually practical to have a party directly after an evening performance so plan a lunch event shortly afterwards.
- Post pictures that were taken during one of the dress rehearsals.
- Make a budget report, deposit the ticket money, and make any reimbursements needed.
- Students from the audience can write reviews as part of their language or drama course. Post the best ones with the photos.

JOBS NEEDED TO PRODUCE A SUCCESSFUL PLAY

Director
The director is the person who helps choose the play and creates a vision of the play based on their understanding of what the play is about. They decide who will be in it and run all the rehearsals. The director also consults with volunteers about the set design, costumes, lighting etc. Although all other jobs should be delegated to someone else, the director is responsible for finding those people.

Backstage Crew
The backstage crew change the sets, have props readily accessible, and are in charge of the curtains and backstage lights. These can be responsible older students, or if rehearsals are after school, you can use high school students.

Bookkeeper
They help plan the budget and keep track of all the money spent.

Choreographer
A choreographer is a person who creates and teaches the dances. This can be a teacher, parent volunteer, older student with dance experience, or high school volunteer. If you can't find someone who wants to choreograph the whole show split up the dance numbers among a few people.

Costumes
A teacher or parent needs to coordinate the making, finding and collection of costumes. Students should bring in their costumes a few weeks before the dress rehearsal. Find a safe place to store them, preferably on a clothing rack with the actor's name marked on each item of clothing.

Hair and Makeup
Most productions at the primary and junior level don't require special hair or makeup. If it is necessary, parent volunteers will be needed.

Lighting
This includes the house and stage lights. Many elementary schools don't have a stage with theatre lights so more than likely it will be having someone turn the lights off and on. An older, responsible student can do this. If the stage area has a series of theatre lights above it, check well in advance if any of the bulbs need to be replaced or if the lights need to be repositioned.

Music Director
The music director is the person responsible for teaching the songs, conducting the music if there is a band, or providing piano accompaniment for musicals. Many musicals come with two CDs; one with practice tracks, music and words, and the other with karaoke or instrumental tracks. It is perfectly acceptable and much easier to have the cast sing along to instrumental tracks for performances. Do not have them perform to the practice tracks. The parents want to hear the students singing, not someone from a studio. If you don't have someone to teach the songs, ask homeroom teachers to play the CD during class time.

Posters
Older students can design these as part of the language or arts curriculum. If there is time, have a contest for the best poster. You can either make copies of the winning poster to use or pick the best ten to post around your school.

The poster should include the following:
- name of the play
- art work
- playwright and composer
- place being held
- time and date
- cost of admission,
- where to buy tickets
- who to contact for information.

For security reasons, it is not recommended to put student names on it.

Program
A program, or a printed leaflet that details various aspects of the performance, should be made to give to the audience. This is important because it acknowledges the students and their roles and gives credit and thanks to all the helpers. It is also a souvenir for the parents. It doesn't need to be more than a letter-sized piece of paper folded in half.

The following should be included in the program:
- the name of the play, playwright and composer;
- the date and location;
- a list of all characters and who is playing each part;
- names of students in the chorus;
- and a list of all helpers and what their job is.

Props
Props are the smaller items used by characters that are necessary to the scene such as an umbrella or book. A teacher or parent volunteer can supervise the collection of these, and the backstage crew will be responsible for making sure they are where they need to be during performances. Have one or two tables in the wings to put props on for actors using them to pick up on their way onstage.

Runner
A runner is the person during a performance who goes to the waiting rooms to let actors know that their cue is coming up, as well as delivering any messages for performance issues that might come up.

Set
The set consists of all the pieces of furniture and scenery that are used on stage to set the scene. A teacher or parent needs to supervise the making or finding of these items. Students can help paint scenery.

Sound
Sound is anything that makes a noise that doesn't come from an actor or a prop. This includes sound effects, CD music tracks, and microphones. The sound person will order what is needed beforehand and operate the soundboard or CD player for performances. Unless you have a very responsible older student with tech experience, it is recommended you use a teacher or parent for this job.

Stage Manager
The stage manager coordinates everything that happens backstage and ensures that things are running smoothly during rehearsals and performances.

Supervisors
Adults are needed to supervise students during rehearsals and productions. One or two adults during full rehearsals should be enough. During performances, you will need someone backstage, someone in the hall, and someone in each of the waiting rooms.

Tickets
You have three choices for admittance to your performance.
1. Charge admission. This will help cover your costs. This also makes sure that you don't exceed the legal number of audience members permitted in the space. Tickets can be made on the computer and then printed off.
2. Don't charge admission. This can cause complications as you will have no idea how many people, if any, plan on coming. Even if there is no charge, you might want to issue free tickets so that you know how many people to expect.
3. Ask for a donation. Make it free but ask for a donation to somewhere such as the food bank. Or make it a free will offering where people pay what they can afford.

THINGS TO CONSIDER
Backstage Etiquette
Certain things are expected from people, either helping or waiting for their cues, who are backstage. Some of these are listed below:
- no talking unless necessary;
- move quietly;
- be ready for your entrances;
- don't distract your fellow cast members who are on stage;
- don't stand in the way;
- be polite to everyone;
- don't touch or move the props unless instructed to;
- don't be backstage unless you are required to be there.

Blocking
Blocking is when the director instructs the actors where and when to move. Some things to keep in mind when blocking are:
- Don't have characters move unless there is a reason to.

- Don't have a character stay standing in the same spot for the whole scene.
- Have the majority of the action take place in the front half of the stage. The closer to the audience the better.
- Keep in mind the sight lines. If there is a pillar on the stage and the actor is standing beside it, can everyone in the audience see them? A rule of thumb is, if the actor can't see everyone in the audience, then everyone in the audience can't see them.
- Don't have actors speak with their back to the audience. They should always have at least part of their face showing when speaking.
- If two or more actors are crossing the stage, have the shorter person closest to the audience. If a group of dancers are on stage, place shorter people in front of the group.
- Don't have an actor exit to the right if they need to come back on stage from the left.
- When grouping actors, don't have them stand in a straight line unless there is a reason for it. Instead, have them stand in triangle formation or at different levels.

Commitment

It is very frustrating to hold a rehearsal only to find out half the characters are missing. Illness is one thing, but if they don't show up because of other reasons, then it can be a problem. Have parents and students sign a commitment agreement, so everyone knows right from the beginning what is expected from them. Students should be responsible for informing the director in advance when they will be absent so that scene work can be rearranged.

Lagging enthusiasm

If during rehearsals enthusiasm is lagging, try changing up the way lines are read. This can be done by:
- reading the lines as rappers, or like you're in a snowstorm;
- sitting in a circle and saying the lines as fast as possible;
- improvising the whole play where the key points are covered while staying in character.

Making money

Should you sell tickets? If you need to cover costs, then yes. The decision to sell tickets and how much they will be should be made by the administration. If you have an intermission, you might consider making additional money by selling snacks and gift items or having a silent auction.

Number of performances

It is up to the school how many performances you have. Most of the time it will be one or two. The audience will consist mostly of family members, so you won't have strangers queuing up to buy tickets. Figure out how many seats you can legally have in your performance space and how many family members per cast member might attend. If this will fill one night, then stop at that. There is nothing more discouraging than performing for a half-empty hall.

Off book
Off book refers to the date when actors are no longer permitted to use their scripts at rehearsals. Because acting involves the whole body the sooner you are not holding a script the sooner you can focus on the acting. The faster this happens, the more confident the actors will be at performance time. Announce the off-book date on the first day of rehearsals. Be firm on this date, which should be mid-way through practices. There will always be students who procrastinate and don't learn their lines. It only takes one rehearsal where they stand awkwardly on stage to make them come back better prepared.

At first, actors may improvise or paraphrase lines to cover up forgotten lines. This is fine and is an excellent skill for actors to develop for when they can't remember their lines during a performance. But it is not something to be encouraged on a regular basis as it changes the verbal cues that other actors rely on to speak their own lines.

Prompters
A prompter is a person who discreetly hides off stage to cue lines to actors who forget them during a performance. It is more professional and promotes a stronger performance if you don't use a prompter. If students know right from the start that there will not be a prompter and you teach them how to cover up mistakes and forgotten lines then one is not necessary, even for the primary grades. Students are capable of remembering lines, and if no one is there to assist them, they won't rely on that assistance, instead relying on the support of their fellow actors.

Scheduling the play
When scheduling the performance dates, check the school schedule to avoid conflicts. Post the dates you select on the school calendar so that when people are scheduling things such as sports day, they don't book the same day.

Scripts
As part of the licensing agreement, you will need to buy scripts for the actors to use. Some agreements allow you to make copies of the scripts after you have purchased a certain number of them. Keep in mind that unauthorized duplication of plays is illegal so check the fine print before doing so. If you are permitted to make copies give the actors with the smaller roles copies of their parts only. For example, copy just the music for the chorus. This will cut down on your photocopy costs as well as save paper.

Waiting Rooms
Before and during performances students will need somewhere to wait. Choose rooms that are close to the stage. The number of rooms required will depend on the size of the cast and how many costume changes there are. Chorus members and actors with smaller parts can change into their costumes in the washroom and then all wait together in one room. Main characters should be in a separate room closest to the stage. If they are on stage for most of the play, they can wait quietly backstage in between their scenes. Otherwise, they can return to their room. Try not to have more than 20 students per room to help keep the noise and nerves down. Plan in advance where students will be, have doors well marked with the names of cast members who should be in that room, and have supervisors either for each room or who will patrol the halls.

WHERE TO BUY PLAYS

If you are doing a musical the best place to buy the script and music is at a local music store that sells educational products. That way you can read the script before purchasing. If you don't have a local music store that has a decent selection of scripts, you can order online directly from a publisher or a music store website.

These are some publishing companies for plays and musicals.

Alfred Music
http://www.alfred.com

Pioneer Drama Service
http://www.pioneerdrama.com

AUDITION FORM

Name: _____

Grade: _____ Homeroom teacher: _____

What part are you interested in? (circle as many as you like)

    chorus   singing solo   main part   small part

    dancer   part with no lines   backstage helper

What talents do you have? i.e. dancing, magic tricks, comedian, play an instrument etc?
_____

What plays have you been in before? What part did you have?
_____

For the director to fill out:

Volume	1	2	3
Clarity	1	2	3
Singing	1	2	3
Expression	1	2	3
Acting	1	2	3

Notes: (parts you might consider them for, overall impressions, behaviour issues etc.)
_____
_____

A checklist for putting on a play

Before rehearsals:
- Choose a play
- Order scripts
- Book the dates
- Announce auditions
- Hold auditions
- Cast the parts
- Post the cast list
- Make a rehearsal schedule and book all rooms needed
- Send rehearsal schedule home
- Book a dress rehearsal

Find people to be:
- backstage crew
- choreographer
- stage manager
- music director
- costume coordinator
- hair and makeup coordinator
- lighting crew
- runners
- sound technician
- supervisors

Find people to make:
- posters/programs
- props
- the set
- tickets
- costumes

Post-performance:
- clean up the stage and waiting rooms
- return props, costumes, and set pieces
- thank volunteers and students
- cast party
- submit budget report

CHAPTER SIXTEEN
Starting a Drama Club

Drama clubs are a great way to expand on your drama program outside of class time with the flexibility for students to create and perform what they wish.

STARTING OUT
Following are things for people to think about if interested in starting a drama club:
- Are there students who are interested?
- What will the focus of the club be? Improv and theatre games? Playwriting? Performance?
- Are there people to assist with running the club? Parent volunteers or older students? Perhaps the local high school has theatre students who need their volunteer hours. Adults or high school students from outside the teacher community may have some skills to add to your repertoire such as dance, lighting, or set construction experience.
- How much time do you have to commit?
- What time or day works best for you and the students? Try to avoid game days to encourage more students to take part. If the club is after school will it be a challenge getting bused students picked up when it is over?
- How many students can join? Likely the club will start small, but if there is only one supervisor, there might need to be a maximum enrolment.
- Who can join? What age group?
- How can you promote the club to gather interest?
- Is there a budget? The amount of money allocated will determine the type of program that can be done. Many drama activities don't require money to run, however, if you wish to work towards a play some money will be necessary.

THE PROGRAM
Some suggestions for what students can do in drama club are:
- Have a collection of fun drama games, improv, scene work, or playwriting that will help to build drama skills but are not directly connected to the curriculum.
- Put on a musical or one-act play where everyone in the club is involved in some capacity. Club time can be used for rehearsals.
- If your club is running year-round, students can do a combination of games and a play.
- Or have a focus on one area, which can change each term or year such as playwriting or developing a theatre sports league.

Do you need to be a drama expert to run a drama club? Absolutely not. A love of theatre and working with students will get you far. Use any of the games from Chapter Fourteen or ideas from Chapter Eighteen to build your program. And if you wish to put on a play or musical all the steps needed to accomplish that are in Chapter Fifteen.

CHAPTER SEVENTEEN
Before the Curtain Closes

MISCELLANEOUS ITEMS ABOUT DRAMA

Beyond the Curriculum
At the end of every assignment where guided learning and instructions have taken place, allow the student to create their version with no restrictions other than their imaginations. For example, students are told they are going to write a commercial based on healthy living, must be one-minute long, have a slogan, and be geared towards a young audience. After that assignment is finished, allow students to create a commercial about anything they want using whichever learned elements they choose. This can be for bonus points or not graded at all, but by giving students the chance to apply what they have learned to their own ideas it encourages their personal creative journey.

Drama Sharing Day
If your students aren't taking part in a school musical or play and therefore won't have the opportunity to perform for their parents, consider having a drama sharing day. This can be as informal as performances in the classroom to a formal event in the auditorium.
   Following are some suggestions for organizing such an event.
- Decide which classes will take part.
- Choose drama works that show a variety of drama skills the students have learned such as improvisation, role-playing, creating a silent movie, or theatre games.
- Have narrators briefly explain what each drama form is before it is performed.
- Make sure every student has a chance to perform without centring the attention on just a few students.
- Time the whole event to fit into your allotted schedule, approximately an hour in length, and practice using a timer.
- Make a schedule so the students will know when they are performing.
- Have a runthrough before the parents come.
- Review the expectations for students when they are not performing.
- If performing improvs or games have a clear signal, such as a bell or horn, to notify students an activity is over.
- With everyone on stage, finish with a group activity that can include the audience, and then take a bow.

Field Trips
If you have a professional theatre company within an hour's drive, it is worthwhile to take a field trip to see a play. Many companies have a student program where they perform a shorter version of a current play, offer backstage tours, have question and answer periods with the actors, and sometimes have interactive performances with the students.
   Some of the values of going to a professional theatre are:
- It gets students excited about live theatre and inspires them in their creations and performances.
- Students can see a professional theatre.

- Students can make connections between professional and amateur theatre.
- It provides opportunities to evaluate and discuss the elements of drama performed by professionals.
- Sometimes a play is a direct connection to a literary work, or time in history, being studied.

Guest Speakers

Invite someone from the local theatre community to give a presentation or teach a drama workshop. A play writer can walk students through the process from what inspired them to what it's like having your play produced. An actor can share experiences that will help students overcome things such as stage fright. Someone from the business end can speak about employment opportunities.

How Communities Benefit from Drama

Theatres provide not only arts and cultural activities, but they also bring revenue to a community. People going to the theatre often eat at nearby restaurants, shop at the local stores, use public transit or parking etc. Many jobs are enhanced by someone with a drama background such as video game developers, teachers, ministers, politicians, or therapists.

Overhead Spotlights

To make a spotlight for classroom performances place a piece of paper with a large circle cut out of it onto an overhead projector. This will project a spotlight onto the wall.

Timer

At the start of an activity tell students how long they have to prepare an assignment, and how long their performance should be. Give them a certain amount of time to plan and then have them practice to a timer so they can edit or add material. Place the timer where they can see and hear it.

CHAPTER EIGHTEEN
Drama Ideas for Lessons Based on the Drama Curriculum

This chapter contains ideas for teaching the various requirements of the drama curriculum. Each activity has a recommended grade level along with the drama skills that it develops.

A DAY IN THE LIFE OF (GRADE 1-3)
- Students will choose a person or object from their life such as a parent, sister, teacher, dog, doll, or bike.
- They will make a list of four to eight key things done by that person or object in a typical day. This can be done using words, drawings, or a combination of both.
- Using a maximum of one minute, students will act out each activity for a few seconds and then move on to the next one in sequence until the portrayed day is complete.
- As the students become more advanced, encourage them to add more details such as showing the time of day or where they are.

Here is an example of what the student's list might look like.
Chosen person—mother
1. wake up
2. make breakfast for everyone
3. drive kids to school
4. go to work
5. make dinner
6. put kids to bed
7. go to sleep

Grade 4-6: This activity can be extended to be used in older grades by following the instructions above to show the day in the life of someone real or imaginary studied in social studies. For example, a blacksmith, King Arthur or the first Olympian.

Drama Skills:
Character Development
Personal connections to their lives and community and life in the past and present
Sequencing of events

ACT YOUR AGE: (GRADE 4-6)

Write in large letters the four stages of life: infancy, childhood, adolescence, and adulthood on four separate pieces of 8 by 10 paper. Students in small groups will begin an improvisation based on an everyday activity. As you hold up a piece of paper, the students must change their behaviour according to the stage of life written on it.

An example would be:

Students begin an improvisation as themselves eating breakfast at a table. The teacher holds up the paper that says INFANCY. Students switch to acting like babies throwing food on the ground, crying etc. When the ADOLESCENCE card is held up, actors continue eating while texting and ignoring others at the table.

Drama skills:
Character development

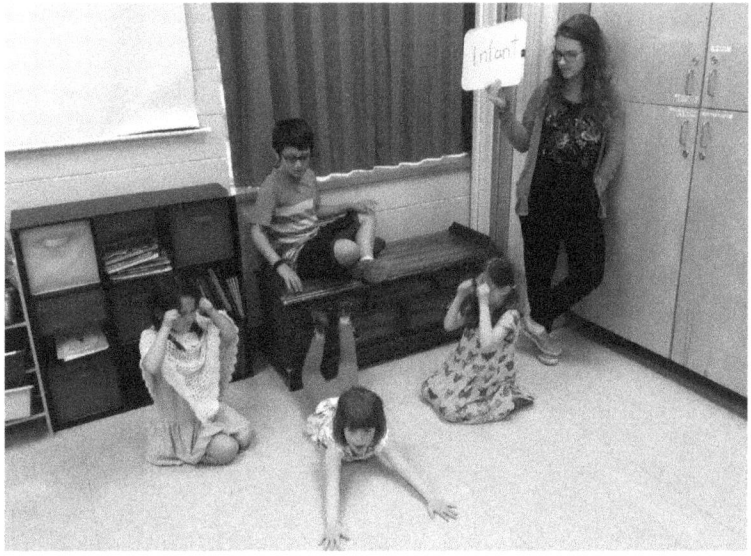

Act Your Age (Photo: Sarah Stubbs)
Activity: Cleaning your room
Stage of life: Infant

ADVICE HALLWAY (GRADE 1- 6)

The purpose of the advice hallway is to explore options for making decisions related to drama works.

Begin by asking students to make two lines that face each other. This can be done anywhere but doing it in the hall gives the students more space. A person states a problem (or the teacher can provide one) and then walks down the middle of the two lines with students on both sides offering their opinions and suggestions as they pass by. At the end of the row, the person states the solution they will use.

Examples of questions could be:
    Playwriting: What should happen next?
    Character study: Why did he do that?
    Life decisions: Should I skip school?
    Conflict management: What should the bullied person do?

For Grade 4 to 6 do this exercise with the two rows of students representing two different perspectives or sides to a problem. For example, stealing. One side would give reasons why you shouldn't steal, with the other line saying why you should.

Drama Skills:
Developing Creativity
Point of view
Problem-solving

AND THEN THIS HAPPENED... (GRADE 1-3)
Someone starts telling a story to the class, either based on a published book or one that is improvised. After thirty seconds, or when there is a pause, the teacher or leader will say, "And then this happened..." Choose someone to replace the first student. They will then continue the story from where the first person left off. Repeat this process until the story is finished.

Drama Skills:
Develop Creative Ideas
Retelling stories

ANIMAL CRACKERS (KINDERGARTEN-GRADE 1)
Buy a box of animal crackers making sure that there are enough crackers for each student to have one. Students will pull out a cookie and act out that animal in front of the class. When students guess which animal they are the actor sits down, eats their cookie, and the next student takes their turn. For larger classes, more than one student can perform at a time.

Note: Gluten-free versions are available in health food stores if there are students with allergies in the class. Gummy animals can also be used.

Drama Skills:
Building confidence performing in front of people

ART GALLERY (GRADE 3-6)
1. Individual students, or small groups, will choose a painting that has the same number of subjects portrayed in it as are in the group. The painting can be by any artist, or an artist from a period students are studying.
2. Students will make a frame for their painting from found materials or draw one on a large piece of paper.
3. They will re-create the painting by posing within the frame wearing similar clothing to what was worn in the painting. Props may also be used.
4. Create a gallery of the re-created paintings along any available wall. Invite parents or other classes to come to a "black tie" gallery opening to view the paintings. Juice and snacks can be served. Any students who are not part of a painting can play the role of a gallery owner, artist, or tour guide.
5. Provide guests a few minutes to view the paintings. Students will hold their positions within the frame during that time. Large colour copies of the original paintings can be posted beside each frame.

Extensions:
6. Once paintings have been viewed invite guests to be seated while students give a short presentation about their paintings.
7. After freezing in position for fifteen seconds, students can perform a written skit either based on fact or fiction showing what the subjects of the painting are doing in the art scene.

Drama Skills:
Costumes
Creating and performing short drama works for specific purposes and audiences
Focus/ stay in role

Art Gallery (Painting: Gaston Lenthe, 1805-60; Photo: Jackie Bennett)
Portrait of a girl with dog

AUDIENCE CHAMELEON (GRADE 1-2)

Depending on where you are there is a protocol for expected behaviour from the audience. With the class brainstorm different places you can be an audience and make a list of them. Some examples would be in the classroom, at an assembly, at church, in the cinema, or at a hockey game.

Choose a couple of the examples from the list to discuss the expected behaviour from the audience during that event. For instance, at a hockey game yelling, cheering, and applauding are all acceptable audience behaviours.

You will then call out one example at a time from the list. The whole class together will do an improv to show what they would look like if they were the audience at that event. After finishing the list, each student will choose two of the listed events and make a written comparison of the similarities and differences. This can be done using a Venn diagram.

Drama Skills:
Good audience skills
Personal connections to their lives and community

AUDITION IMPROVISATION (GRADE 1-6)

There are many ways to hold auditions. This is an example of one way that is simple and requires no preparation from the students. This can also be used outside of auditions for a quick, fun activity to help students build their confidence in performing.

Choose ten character types and emotions that will be needed in the play you are casting and write each one on a separate 8-in. by 10-in. card. For example, for the musical *The Princess and the Pea*, you could use the words happy, sad, angry, scared, rap, king, evil, princess, diva, and joker. As each actor stands up to audition, they will say or sing a nursery rhyme or song of their choosing that they know from memory. Hold up each of the cards randomly throughout their performance. As each card is shown, they will change how they are performing the song to adapt to the word.

An example would be:
- A student recites the nursery rhyme "Mary Had A Little Lamb."
- The actor says in their natural voice, "Mary had a little lamb."
- You hold up the word angry, and the student continues with, "his fleece is white as snow" in an angry tone.
- Hold up rapper, and they continue as a rapper saying, "everywhere that Mary went the lamb was sure to go."
- The student will repeat their song until all cue cards have been used. If the person shows no diversity, you only need to have them go through the song twice.

Ask an experienced student to model this for the students before auditions begin. Practice a run through with the whole group and then proceed with auditioning students one at a time. If students are particularly nervous, they can perform in pairs. (See YouTube video for an example of an audition improvisation.)

Drama Skills:
Building confidence in performing in front of people
Developing vocal and facial expressions
Focus/ staying in role

BACK AND FORTH (GRADE 4-6)

1. Students will choose a character the same age as themselves, either real or fictional, from a time in history being studied in class. For example, if a boy is learning about medieval times, he could choose a stable boy as his character.
2. They will then make a list of the things done in a typical day that would be similar and different to themselves and their character.
3. Provide the students with a template showing two picture frames or have them draw their own. They will draw a picture of what they might have looked like then and another showing what they look like now. Similarities and differences can be written in point form round the pictures. A Venn diagram can be used as well.
4. Ask students to create and perform a short drama work where they clearly show similarities and differences while performing an activity in current time, time travel to the past to continue what they were doing, and then travel back to modern time.

The student can go back and forth as many times as they like within the given time restrictions while showing changes to their character. Costumes and props can be used.

Drama Skills:
Creating and presenting
Developing creativity
Elements of drama: role and character, time and place
Make personal connections

BUILD A SCENE (GRADE 1-3)

This is an improvisation exercise that begins with one person on stage, with additional students added as a scene is developed. The scene should be based on a connection to their lives but can have fictitious elements.

An example of this would be:

Situation: A boy is scared to skate because he thinks he might fall.
1. A boy begins the scene. He might say things while wobbling on the ice such as, "If I skate, I might fall down and break my leg. Maybe my brother can help me." He taps, or points, to a male student in the audience.
2. That student joins the improv by playing the big brother. "I ate too much pizza and think I might be sick if I skate right now. Ask the giraffe for help."
3. A person playing a giraffe enters the scene.
4. Add as many characters as possible until the scene resolves itself, the time limit has been reached, or the scene has reached a dead end.

Drama Skills:
Developing creativity
Personal connections to their lives and community
Role-play

CHANGE (GRADE 1-3)

In small groups have students act out a familiar fairy tale or story. When they get to a pivotal point, the teacher will say, "change the _____." You can say change the ending, character, hero, location etc. From that point, students will improvise what happens next.

Things for actors to consider:

Character and Relationship:
If you became a different character how would the story change? Would someone else become the hero? In the story of Red Riding Hood, if the woodsman didn't come who else might have saved Red Riding Hood? Someone else in the story? Or would someone else need to be added?

Time and Place:
If Grandma lived in the present day, how would the story change?

Drama Skills:
Building confidence performing in front of people
Develop creativity
Elements of drama—role/relationship/time and place
Retelling stories

CHANGE THE MEANING: WORD EMPHASIS (GRADE 1-6)
In small groups, students will pick a phrase such as, "I want that ice cream please." By emphasizing different words, the meaning of the sentence will change. For example, "**I** *want* that ice cream please" indicates the speaker feels they should get the ice cream whereas, "I want *that* ice cream please" shows that they want a particular flavour. Groups will create a short scene using their chosen phrase as many ways possible within the drama work.

Drama Skills:
Developing vocal expression
Elements of drama- role
Interpretation
Point of view

CHANGE THE MOOD (GRADE 4-6)
Students will plan and perform a one-minute skit about something curriculum- or age-related. Students will present their skit a second time, this time changing one of the elements of drama to create a different mood. The teacher can either assign the element to be used, or students can choose their own. Students not only will change an element of drama but also need to show how it changes the story. After presenting the skit different ways discuss how the changes affected the story and decide which is preferred and why.

An example of this would be a skit about a person going to a sleepover. The first run through could be about a girl who is excited because she will be spending the night with all of her friends and everything goes wonderfully.

On the second run, the following could be changed:

The element of character:
The character now becomes someone who is scared they will not be near their parents.

The element of time:
The skit now takes place in pioneer time.

The element of tension:
Play scary music and dim the lights before leaving home.

Drama Skills:
Develop creativity
Elements of drama
Presenting

DRAMA IDEAS FOR LESSONS BASED ON THE DRAMA CURRICULUM

CHANGE THE MOOD 2 (GRADE 1-3)
Using your voice and body language can change the meaning of a sentence.
1. Create six 8-in. by 10-in. cue cards with a different emotion printed on each one.
2. Each student will think of a short sentence such as, "I love goldfish."
3. Taking turns, students will stand up and say their sentence, each time changing the way the phrase is said according to the cue card you hold up. For example, if you hold up a card with the word angry written on it, the student might yell that they love goldfish with their arms tightly folded across their chest. Do this with the other five cards.
4. When everyone has had the chance to perform discuss how the mood changed depending on the emotional response.

Drama Skills:
Interpretation
Building confidence performing in front of people
Developing vocal expression and body language

Change the Mood 2 (Photo: Sarah Stubbs)
Emotion: Happy
Activity: Writing a test

CHARACTER DEVELOPMENT (GRADE 1-6)
Character development is used to create believable characters in drama works as well as when learning to act. Following are the curriculum-suggested areas of character development explored at each grade that can be incorporated into written and performance-based assignments. Each level builds on what was learned in previous years.

Grade 1: show how a character is feeling.
Grade 2: use voices and emotions to show a character's point of view.
Grade 3: demonstrate the point of view of more than one character.
Grade 4: develop characters while remaining focused in a role.
Grade 5: explore the inner and outer life of a character.
Grade 6: develop characters with an awareness of stereotypes.

Drama Skills:
Character development

CHARACTER ON THE WALL (GRADE 1-6)
(See Chapter Eleven for a detailed lesson plan and completed character drawing.)

1. Read a short story or play to the class.
2. Using a large piece of paper, the length of a student, trace around a student, being careful to include all details such as the shoes, ponytail, fingers etc. Do not cut out the shape, or if you do, leave a large border for students to write on.
3. Make one of these tracings for each of the main characters in the story and post them around the classroom.
4. Ask students to write on the paper things they know about the character either within the body or to the side of it. For example, if you have chosen the story, "Jack and the Beanstalk," write "Jack" at the top of one of the drawings. On the head, you might write "brown hair" and on the feet write, "too poor to own shoes." At the side of the outline, you could put, "lives in a forest a long time ago," etc. Add any known characteristics such as age, gender, likes/dislikes, secrets, or personality traits.
5. This exercise can be done for short stories, plays, novel studies, or for getting to know students at the beginning of the year.

Drama Skills:
Character development
Elements of drama - role

CHARACTER, PLACE, AND ME (GRADE 4-6)
- Give each student three pieces of paper large enough to write one word on it.
- On the first piece of paper they will write their name, on the second a location such as an amusement park, moon, or shopping centre, and on the third they will write a character, either real or fictitious.
- Put each category into three different containers, ensuring the categories are not mixed.
- Pull out a student's name first. The student has the opportunity to accept the challenge or decline, but once they accept, they can't change their mind if they don't like the character they are given. Next, pull out a character name for the student. Repeat this with three other students, assigning a character to each of them.
- Then pull out one piece of paper with a location. The improv will then be performed by those four students.

An example of this is:
> Four students, Katica, Bristol, Johnston, and Ravon, have their names drawn. Katica will be Shrek; Bristol will be Cinderella; Johnston will be a pilot; and Ravon will be the King of England. The location is a swimming pool. The four students will do a short improvisation of their characters at the pool.
>
> If students are having difficulty thinking of storylines throw scenarios at them such as a shark in the pool or a flock of pigeons landing on their heads to keep the action moving.

Drama Skills:
Building confidence performing in front of people
Developing creativity
Elements of drama

CHARACTER SKETCH (GRADE 4-6)
Before beginning scene work, or a production, have students create a written character sketch for the role they are playing, regardless of whether they have a lead part or not. Either assign five questions to ask about their character or have them create their own. Sample questions could be:
- What word best describes your character's personality?
- Does your character like what they do?
- Is your character liked? Why or why not?

Students should answer as accurately as possible, but if there is not enough information available to do so, then students can make an educated guess.

Drama Skills:
Character development
Elements of drama: role

CHORAL READING (GRADE 1-6)
Choral reading is the telling of a story in unison by a group of people. This exercise can be done as a class or in small groups.

1. The teacher will choose a poem or short story that has lots of possibilities to add dynamics and sound effects.
2. Read the poem or story through as a group to ensure all words are familiar.
3. Brainstorm areas that can use sound effects, dynamics, or movement and decide which ones will be used.
4. Practice as a group. As you would do with a choir, all inflections, dynamics, etc. need to be the same so that no one stands out. In Grade 4 and up you can add the occasional solo if it helps to further the story. Perform the story, either memorized or reading from a script, at an assembly or for another class.

Drama Skills:
Building confidence performing in front of people
Developing creativity
Developing vocal expression

Drama forms
Retelling stories

COMMERCIALS (GRADE 1-6)
(See Chapter Eleven for a detailed lesson plan.)
Individually, or in small groups, create commercials to advertise a real or imaginary product or service with the intended buyer in mind. Ads can be used in any subject that students need to demonstrate knowledge about. Some examples of commercials could be:
- an all-inclusive trip to Ancient Greece
- stone wheels for carts
- pioneer dolls for Christmas
- jousting lessons

Drama Skills:
Creating short drama works for specific purposes and audiences
Develop creativity

CONFLICT RESOLUTION FAIRY (GRADE 1-3)
In groups of 3 or more come up with a problem that has been experienced at school. Role play the conflict showing two points of view. After about a minute the Confliction Resolution Fairy (CRF), dressed in wings and a wand, steps forward and offers a conflict resolution. This activity can be done as an entire lesson with as many conflicts as can be considered or as a quick exercise to deal with an immediate conflict.

If students are too mature to play the part of a fairy, brainstorm with the class a name they are comfortable with. For example, conflict resolution robot or a made-up name. The idea is to show both sides of a conflict with a third-party arbitrator helping to arrive at a solution both parties are happy with.

If this exercise is practiced enough, students will be able to use this skill by themselves outside of the classroom. Consider teaching this concept to older students who can then take turns taking on the role during recesses where younger students can come to them for help solving conflicts.

Extension: Choose a conflict experienced by a character in a story, such as the giant being angry at Jack for coming into his home uninvited, and create a short scene where the CRF becomes involved.

Drama Skills:
Point of view
Role play to explore solutions to everyday problems

CONSEQUENCES (GRADE 1-6)
The purpose of this exercise is to look at the effect wrongful actions have on the victim and to see the event from their point of view.
1. In small groups, students will choose an act that is wrong, either something that is not a chargeable offence, such as being mean to your sibling, or is, such as stealing.
2. Brainstorming amongst themselves they will discuss possible consequences of the wrongful action.

For an example of this kind of exercise, imagine that a rock was thrown at a window and that the window was broken.

Possible consequences of that action could be:
- A cat on the other side of the window gets cut.
- The elderly lady who lives there is worried because she doesn't know how she will pay for the broken window.
- The lady now feels scared living in her house and fears someone might try to break in.

3. A skit will be created that clearly shows a wrongful action followed by the effects that action has on the victim. At the conclusion of the scene, restitution will be offered such as to pay for the window repair, apologize to the lady, or volunteer to help around the house. The restitution can be suggested by any of the characters in the scene.
4. Students will perform their skit for the class.

The wrongful acts used in these skits should be age-appropriate.

Drama Skills:
Consequences for actions
Creating short drama works for specific purposes
Point of view

CREATE A CHARACTER (GRADE 1-6)
This is an improvisation exercise where the teacher assigns a setting, and students create a scene using characters that would belong there.

In Grade 1, locations can be from the student's community. In higher grades, settings can be drawn from books students have read, periods in history that they are studying or places they have not visited.

Scenes should be no longer than two minutes.

Here are some examples of settings as well as of the characters that might be found in such settings:

- **Grocery store:** shop workers, parents and their kids, or delivery people.
- **Arena:** attendant, Zamboni driver, skater or coach.
- **Pioneer village:** teacher, farmer, blacksmith or doctor.
- **Magical forest:** trolls, unicorns, lost warrior or fairies.

Drama Skills:
Creating short drama works
Developing creativity
Elements of drama- character, time and place
Personal connections

CULTURAL CELEBRATIONS (GRADE 1-6)
A cultural celebration is one of the many ways students can learn about cultural diversity. This event can consist of short presentations done in class or an all-day celebration expanded to include the school community.

Ideas for what can be included in a cultural celebration are given below.
1. Students will plan and prepare presentations. Here are some examples of what can be done:
    - cultural dances that are performed or taught to include the audience
    - sing or play traditional songs
    - skits or short plays
    - art show
    - clothing then and now
    - PowerPoint presentations or speeches
    - storytelling from around the world
    - posters showing various traditions, food, clothing, customs, etc.
    - tableaux with small groups showing, "What is Christmas?" "What is Hanukkah?" "What is Chinese New Year?"
2. Host a breakfast or lunch where each student brings a traditional item of food or drink from their country of origin for students to try. Descriptions of each item should be included. Advance organization will cut down on the overabundance of food that potlucks have.
3. Students can wear something traditional from the country their family is originally from. This does not need to be a complete costume as many students will not have access to that. They can wear their countries' colours, create a traditional hairstyle or attach symbols to their shirt.

There are many areas of the curriculum that explore cultural representation and can be included in a cultural celebration. Some of these are:
- Nanabozho and Anansi stories;
- festivals and pageants from different parts of the world;
- myths and stories from different countries;
- Indigenous plays.

Drama Skills:
Creating short drama works for specific purposes
Drama forms
Personal connections
Cultural representation

DIFFERENT PURPOSE (GRADE 4)

Students will brainstorm different uses for an object and present a short skit showing that object being used with its new purpose. These can be things that would actually work such as using a baseball cap to catch fish or made up such as using a flashlight to make spaghetti.

Extension: This also works well as an improvisation exercise. Give the student performing an object they are to include in their story.

Drama Skills:
Developing creativity

DRAMA JOBS (GRADE 5)

Divide the class into groups. Each group will become an expert on one of the different jobs found in the theatre and present their findings to the class. This can be done as a written report, Bristol board presentation, skit, verbal presentation etc. A job description as well as describing a typical day for the professional should be included.

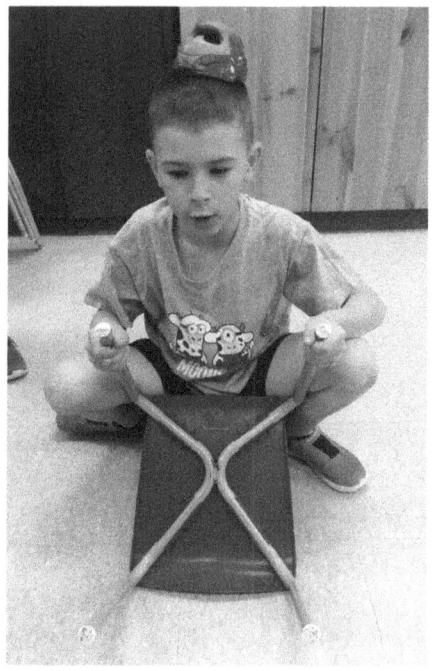

Different Purpose (Photo: Sarah Stubbs)
Found item: Chair
Different Purpose: Go cart

The main jobs are the producer, director, actor, playwright, stage manager, set and costume designers, lighting and sound technician.

Drama Skills:
Creating short drama works for specific purposes and audiences
Learning about careers in the theatre.

DRAMA JOURNALS (GRADE 4-6)

Drama journals can be used for students to keep track of ideas, to reflect and analyze drama works, respond to guided questions, store assignments, record group work, etc.

Drama Skills:
To document the various stages of the creative process

DYNAMICS (GRADE 1)

Dynamics—speed and volume—are important to set the mood of a play. Begin by exploring the different dynamics used in music. A lullaby sung loudly is not effective for helping a baby fall asleep. Singing the national anthem as quickly as possible shows disrespect.

When dynamics are applied to drama works, they also can change the intended meaning. Students will pick a familiar nursery rhyme such as "Mary Had a Little Lamb" and say or sing it using different dynamics to change the mood and purpose of the piece. An emphasis should also be on using facial expression and vocal tone to set the mood.

Drama Skills:
Building confidence performing in front of people
Developing vocal expression
Elements of drama: tension

ESCALATE (GRADE 2-6)
Escalating dialogue by changing the volume and speed is another way to use dynamics to change the mood of a scene.
1. In pairs, students will choose an age-appropriate scenario where an argument or disagreement may result such as not getting a lent item back.
2. A short script will be written and performed where the dialogue causes the mood to change.

Example:
> **Alfredo:** Tamika. Can I have my pencil back that you borrowed?
> **Tamika:** I don't know where it is.
> **Alfredo:** What do you mean? You said you'd give it back.
> **Tamika:** It's just a pencil.
> **Alfredo:** It was my last one. How could you lose it?
> **Tamika:** It's not like I did it on purpose.
> **Alfredo:** You always say you'll return stuff and you don't.
> **Tamika:** That's not true!
> **Alfredo:** Yes it is! I'm never going to trust you again.
> **Tamika:** Fine. I'll never talk to you again.

As the scene escalates, and emotions run high, the volume and pace of dialogue will naturally increase along with the body language.

3. When the scene is over, discuss what was the cause for the escalation and what could have been done to change the outcome. How did volume and dialogue contribute to altering the mood in the scene?
4. Rewrite the script using different words to change the dynamics and mood of the drama work.
5. Perform the revised work and discuss the changes.

Other scene ideas could be based on approaching a haunted house, sneaking past your teacher when you're late for class, riding on a roller coaster, etc. The key is to choose scenes where the dynamics can naturally change.

Drama Skills:
Developing vocal expression
Developing body language

FAIRYTALE THERAPY (GRADE 2-4)
1. In groups of three, students will choose a fairytale that tells two different points of view.
2. Two of the students will play the parts of the characters with the different points of view such as Cinderella and a stepsister. The third student will play the therapist.

3. Improvise a scene where the two characters have a chance to give their point of view. The therapist will ask questions to help them better understand their issues and possibly resolve them. The depth of response from the person playing the therapist will depend on the grade level. Students in Grade 2 might ask simple questions such as, "Why are you mad?" to more complex questions in older grades such as, "How did that make you feel when Cinderella got more attention from her father than you?"

Drama Skills
Point of View

FAKE IT TILL YOU MAKE IT (GRADE 4-6)
Mistakes will happen during performances. The trick is to continue without the audience knowing. Following is an activity for students to learn how to recover from their mistakes.

The most common mistake during a performance is forgetting lines. Because a cast works together as a team, it is the responsibility of both the person speaking and the others on stage to help get a scene back on track when words are forgotten.

Part One
1. Choose a short scene from a play that has four to six main characters in it. Assign every part but one to students in the class. For example, if there are five characters in the scene cast four of them.
2. Those four students will perform the scene using scripts.
3. Every time there is a line that should be read by the absent fifth person one of the four actors will make up a line to cover the mistake.
   For example:
   The fifth person should have said, "Would anyone like a drink of milk?"
   Someone could say for him, "I'm thirsty. Could I have some milk to drink?"
4. Continue until the scene is finished.

Part Two
1. Choose a short scene from a play no one has read that has four to six main characters in it. Assign all the parts.
2. Choose one of the cast to play the forgetful actor.
3. Run the scene with the forgetful actor deliberately making mistakes such as forgetting lines, skipping ahead, or reading someone else's lines. The actors must react in character, adapt where possible and in such a way as to not let the audience know a mistake has been made.
4. After the scene is completed, ask the audience if and when they noticed any mistakes.
5. Repeat this exercise with a new script and new cast members.
6. Discuss the difficulties the students had with both versions of this activity.

Part Three
1. Choose a short scene from a play that has four to six main characters in it. Assign all the parts.
2. Run through the scene once.
3. Run the scene again but this time choose one or two students from the class to

provide unexpected problems within the scene. This could be things like taking a chair away, turning the lights off, knocking over a set piece, etc. Actors must either act as if they didn't notice the interruption or logically incorporate it into the scene.

Drama Skills:
Building confidence performing in front of people
Developing acting/performing skills
Mistakes while performing

FILM PERFORMANCES (GRADE 4-6)

Film performances, either in the planning process or during a performance, to play back for students to watch and evaluate their own and others' performances. This will provide the opportunity for actors to observe the whole action from the audience's perspective rather than just the slice each person sees in front of them.

Drama Skills:
Analyze, reflect, respond
Peer critiquing

FIVE THINGS TO KNOW ABOUT ME (GRADE 1-6)

This lesson is to help develop quick character sketches based on people from the community or characters from stories.

Part 1

Who Am I? One actor stands in front of the class and shows or tells five things about their chosen character to make people guess who they are without saying their name. For example: 1) I help people 2) I work in a hospital 3) I get annoyed when people leave garbage on the floor, etc. Students can be asked to guess after each clue or after all five have been performed.

Part 2

Once students are comfortable with part one, the reverse can be done. A student will pick a character, real or imaginary, and sit in front of the class. Five students will ask a question about the character to learn more about them. Sample questions could be: What is your job? What is your favourite food? What do you hate doing the most? Would you prefer a goat or an elephant for a pet? etc. In the junior grade, questions should be more advanced such as: What kind of clothes do you wear? What prop would you use to show who you are? How would you show you are angry? etc.

Part 3

Play the popular party game where you tape character names on each person's back. People can see everyone else's character except their own. Students walk around the room asking their classmates questions about their unknown character. When they guess who their character is they will sit down. When everyone is seated, the game is over.

Drama Skills:
Character development
Elements of drama: role, relationship, time and place

FOR REAL (GRADE 1-3)

1. Each student writes on a small piece of paper the name of an object found in the classroom and writes an object not found in the classroom on another piece of paper. Place the classroom objects in one container, and the outside objects in another container.
2. One student will draw a paper from each container. If for example the word *ruler* is drawn from the classroom object box, the student will find a ruler.
3. The student will then draw a piece of paper from the outside box. If for example the word *hamster* is drawn, the actor does an improvisation to convince the class that the ruler is a hamster without disclosing what it is. While holding the ruler close to his face, he could say things such as, "This is Humphrey. He is very friendly, but he sometimes bites me. He spends a lot of time running around in circles and needs his cage cleaned every day, or it starts to stink up the house."
4. The class will guess what the new object is.

Drama Skills:
Building confidence performing in front of people
Developing creativity

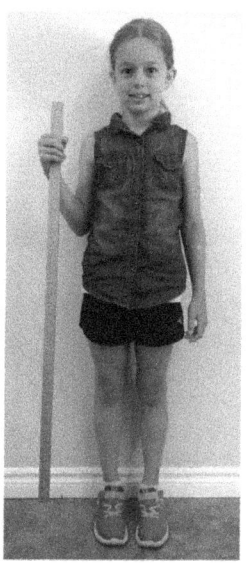
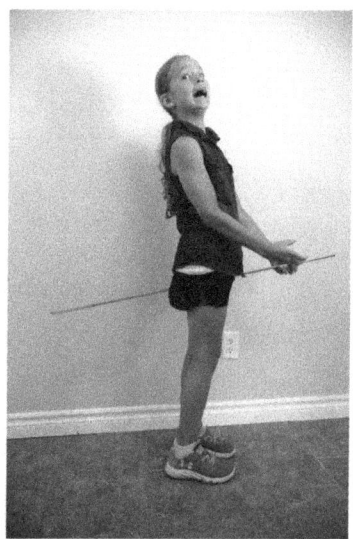

For Real (Photo: Jackie Bennett)
Object found in the classroom: ruler
Object not found in the classroom: witch's broomstick

GOOD AUDIENCE/LISTENER (GRADE K-3)

The main idea is to review what a good listener or audience member looks like.

1. Make two lists, the first being characteristics of a good audience, the second showing listening skills that need to be improved. Headings such as *happy* and *sad* could be used instead of *good* and *bad*. Brainstorm with the class about things to put on each list. For example, being polite, helpful, or hands-on-laps on the happy audience list, and talking, laughing or crawling on the floor on the other list.

2. Put all the valid ideas, both positive and negative, on separate cue cards, illustrated if necessary. This can be done ahead of time as most skills will be universal.
3. Shuffle the cards. Hand out one card each to four students. Choose one person to be the teacher. Model first time through.
4. The "teacher" will stand at the front of the class. Each of the students with a cue card will behave according to their card. The teacher guesses what their cards say. If the teacher is right, then the student stops acting the way the card suggests and sits quietly with the rest of the class.
   An example would be,
   > A student has the card that says "sit with hands on lap" and is doing so. The teacher could say, "Kalila, you are a good listener because you are sitting with your hands on your lap."
5. Keep going until the teacher guesses the four listening behaviours.
6. Shuffle the cards, hand out four of them to four new students and choose a new teacher. Do as many times as time allows or as needed to reinforce the concept of good listening.

Drama Skills:
Developing good audience skills

GREEK THEATRE (GRADE 5)

As part of an ancient civilization unit, students can learn about Greek theatre, which has many components still used today. This knowledge can be presented to the class in a variety of ways such as creating model theatres, performing skits, PowerPoint presentations, etc.
Some of the areas that can be researched are:
- Performance spaces;
- Types of Greek theatre such as tragedy, comedy, satire;
- Playwrights: Sophocles, Aristophanes;
- Role of the chorus and how they perform;
- Performing with masks.

Drama Skills:
Drama forms

GUIDED IMAGERY (K- GRADE 1)

Guided imagery is where a leader describes in detail a scene and the students silently act it out. This can be done for any subject area.
   An example would be the growth of flowers. Students begin curled up on the ground. The leader describes the process as students act it out. "You are a tiny seed, lying under nice soft earth. As water rains down on the soil, you become a small plant, pushing your way out of the seed. You poke at the earth around you until you grow tall enough to push out of the ground." Students continue to act out what is being said until the leader is finished—in this case, when a flower is in full bloom.

Drama Skills:
Building confidence performing in front of people
Developing creativity
Developing body language

GYMNASTIC RIBBONS (K-GRADE 4)
Gymnastic ribbons are a great way to learn about the different moods that music can create. If you don't have access to ribbons, try making them in art class using strips of fabric or paper streamers attached to chopsticks.

Play a selection of songs with various moods and invite students to move around the room using their ribbons according to how the music makes them feel. When finished, discuss their findings and how this would relate to creating moods for dramatic works. Older students can create dance routines using the ribbons.

Drama Skills:
Developing body language
Creating moods

HOT AND COLD (GRADE 1-3)
Write a variety of temperatures on separate pieces of large paper. For Grade 1, write and draw pictures of the four seasons under the appropriate temperature. In small groups, students will begin an improvisation where they are performing an indoor or outdoor activity of their choice. As you hold up a temperature card, they will adjust their drama work to incorporate the new temperature or season. For example, they begin by lawn bowling. When you hold up the card that says minus twenty degrees they continue as they shiver and slip on the ground while they bowl.

Drama Skills:
Improvisation
Personal connections to their lives

HOW CAN YOU SHOW? (GRADE 1-3)
This is a guided exercise to show how you can communicate without using your voice. The teacher or leader will ask an individual or the whole class questions such as, "How can you show you are a friend without saying it?" Students will quickly show their responses by using body language and facial expressions. Each response will last a few seconds before moving on to the next question. This activity can also be useful for getting the class's attention or getting them to settle down.

Other examples are:
- How can you show you love pizza?
- How can you show you are scared of hamsters?
- How can you show you didn't study for a test?
- How can you show compassion to someone who is hurt?

Drama Skills:
Developing vocal expression
Developing facial and body expression

HOW CAN YOU TELL? (GRADE 4-6)
How can you tell is a written or verbal exercise to explain what the elements of drama are in a viewed or read drama work where the answer is not clearly stated. For example, even though it doesn't say that a play takes place in pioneer times, you would know by the costumes and the daily lives of the characters.

Examples of questions that can be used to explore the elements of drama in a dramatic work are:
- How can you tell where the play took place?
- How can you tell who the main character is?
- How can you tell what time of day or year the play took place?
- How can you tell the play was scary?

Drama Skills:
Elements of drama
Interpretation

HOW DO YOU SPEAK? (GRADE 1-2)

In pairs, students will brainstorm how we speak in different scenarios. For example, in a library we whisper, at a soccer game we yell, or on a roller coaster we scream. Each pair will choose a situation and plan a brief skit to perform for the class demonstrating the scenario without mentioning the name of the location where it is taking place. The class will guess where the location is.

Drama Skills:
Developing creativity
Developing vocal expression
Personal connections to their lives and community

HOW WAS YOUR DAY? (GRADE 4-6)

At some point, you might have asked a child how their day was, and you got the standard answer of "OK." Or if you asked, "What did you do today?" you might get "nothing" as an answer. This exercise is to encourage other responses which will lead to improving dialogue in playwriting as well as overall communication.

One person stands at the front of the class. Someone will ask a question about that person's day that needs to be answered truthfully, although students should always know that they are not required to reveal personal details they want to keep private.

When the question has been answered a new student comes to the front who will be asked a new question.

The challenge is to ask questions that will require more than a one-word answer and will provide the most interesting responses. At the end, the class can vote on which was the best question asked.

This is a good game to play at the end of the day.

Some sample questions are:
- What was the funniest thing that happened to you today?
- What was the most interesting thing you learned today?
- If you could redo one thing today what would it be?

Drama Skills:
Developing creativity

HUMAN COMPUTER (GRADE 3)
1. In small groups, students will brainstorm video or computer games they have seen or played.
2. Students will choose an appropriate game they are familiar with. Keeping in mind school behaviour policies, they will recreate it as a short skit that they will perform for their class.
3. After all the skits have been performed the groups will create a new skit where they extend the game to take part in the real world. After these are performed, students will reflect on the differences. How is the story in the game appropriate or not appropriate in reality? What aspects of the story would not work in a real situation?
4. To extend this activity students can be invited to create an original human computer game that is appropriate and realistic to the real world.

Drama Skills:
Developing creativity
Reality versus fiction

IMMIGRATION (GRADE 3-6)
Students will create short skits to recreate what it would be like to immigrate to a new country during a time in history they are studying.

Younger grades can do this as a large group. For example, they are all on a ship together crossing the ocean during the potato famine. The emphasis would be on what it was like to spend months on a boat. Older students can be divided into smaller groups to each recreate their immigration experience, including details such as what led to the decision to make the move, and what were they hoping for in their new country.

Grade 5 extension:
Divide the class into four groups. Assign a different time in history to each group such as 1868, 1920, 2019, and 2090. Each group will research immigration and travel during their assigned date and create a short drama work. Ask the students to present their dramas in order of time, one after each other with no break. Each student will write a brief report discussing the similarities and differences.

Drama Skills:
Personal connections to life in the past and present

IN AND OUT (GRADE 4-6)
In and Out is an exercise used to develop characters and plays, and to solve problems. It involves acting out a situation or developing drama work until you reach a problem. The scene then stops, and the actors step out of role to discuss the situation as themselves. There is a definite separation between how a character behaves and thinks to how the actor does.

An example would be:
Situation: you have lost your mother in the mall.
The teacher says, "In role."
The actor begins a scene as a two-year-old at the mall. Suddenly, he realizes he's lost his mother and panics.
The teacher says, "Out of role."

The action stops and the actor and others watching discuss what the character could do: Don't leave the mall, don't go to a stranger unless they are a police officer, or stay in one place to wait.
The teacher says, "In role."
The scene is continued using the ideas that were discussed.

In and Out can also be used in role playing to solve conflicts.
An example would be:
Situation: A bully wants your money.
The teacher says, "In role."
Students playing the parts of a bully and victim act out a scene with the bully demanding money.
The teacher says, "Out of role."
The actors discuss what could be done in this situation.
The teacher says, "In role."
Continue with the role play using logical solutions to resolve the conflict.

Drama Skills:
Analyze, reflect, respond
Role play: exploring solutions to everyday problems

IN THE MOOD (GRADE 1-3)
Find two pieces of music that have entirely different moods or themes. Listen to the first piece of music. In small groups, students will create one-minute dramas that suit the music and then perform it while the music is playing. They will repeat their drama, this time accompanied by the second song, and will make appropriate changes according to the mood of the music.

For example: Play the song "Walking on Sunshine" while students perform a short skit where they enjoy a day on the beach eating ice cream. Repeat the skit, but this time students might show that they are freezing on the beach while a winter song such as "Frosty the Snow man" is being played.

Extension for Grade 4-6.
Choose the version they like the most and add lights, props, set, costumes, scenery or sound effects to make the scene more effective.

Drama Skills:
Developing creativity
Creating mood
Elements of drama – Grade 4-6 extension

INTERVIEWS/ TALK SHOWS (4-6)
Interviews are a great way to present information, especially using the talk show format, and can cover many expectations from the curriculum.
1. In small groups, students will choose a topic and research facts relating to it.
2. Choose the format best suited to reporting the subject. Will it be an interview on the news where a reporter questions a witness or expert? Or will it be done as a talk show where there is a host interviewing various people who are of interest to the audience?
3. Decide who the characters will be and who will play which part.

4. Write out a list of questions to be asked during the presentation along with their answers. Rehearse and then perform. To achieve a more natural performance, answers do not need to be memorized.

Examples of things the reporter, as part of a news broadcast, would be interviewing someone about:
- the recent volcano in ancient Rome;
- winning an award for inventing the wheel;
- being an athlete in the first Olympics;
- weather conditions in Northern Ontario.

Groups of people that could be guests on a talk show could be:
- a music group from medieval times;
- explorers who have just crossed the ocean to a new land;
- scientists to discuss climate change;
- athletes from the first Olympics;
- doctors to address health concerns;
- people involved in a play.

Drama Skills:
Creating short drama works for specific purposes and audiences
Drama forms

JUDGE (GRADE 5-6)
The purpose of this exercise is to present two sides to a story with a neutral person, the judge, acting as an arbitrator. Set the scene as a courthouse with the judge at the front. Choose a problem such as a bike being borrowed and not returned in good condition. Each side will present their side, and the judge will give an impartial opinion and solution for what should be done to solve the problem. This scene can be scripted or improvised.

Drama Skills:
Creating short drama works for specific audiences and purposes

LARYNGITIS (GRADE 1-3)
One at a time, students will think of a situation where someone needs to tell a story, ask for something, or give instructions but has laryngitis and can't talk. The actor must act out what he needs to say by using props, and body language. This can be done either with the student trying to convey their message to the class or as part of an improv with other actors.

Drama Skills:
Developing body language
Elements of drama

MAKE ME LAUGH (GRADE 1-3)
This is a quick, fun game to help students develop concentration. Have one or two volunteers stand before the class, who will be standing at their desks or in a performance area. The volunteers can do anything appropriate to try and make the rest of the students smile, laugh, or lose concentration without touching them.

For example, they can make funny faces, sounds and movements. As soon as someone shows signs of breaking concentration, such as biting their lip to stop from laughing, that person sits down. Continue until only two people remain. Those two people will now take over as the volunteers, and everyone else will stand up to start another round. Note: Many competitive students will not admit to losing their focus. Sometimes the teacher needs to invite people to sit down when this happens.
(Grade 4-6)
Use this exercise during play rehearsals to help actors practice staying in role when on stage. Actors not in the scene will try to distract those that are.

Drama Skills:
Focus/ stay in role

MAKING TOAST (GRADE 4-5)
(See Chapter Eleven for a detailed lesson plan.)
Sequencing is important for writing all drama works. Give each student a cue card and ask them to write in point form the steps needed to make toast. The teacher will choose several of the cards and step by step follow the instructions exactly as written to make toast.

As most students will forget some of the instructions, they will quickly learn the importance of making sure they include all the steps. Hand back the original cards and ask the students to write on the other side a revised list of instructions. Choose a few cards and follow the more detailed steps to make toast.

Drama Skills:
Developing creativity
Sequencing of events

MANNEQUIN CHALLENGE (GRADE 1-6)
The mannequin challenge is a modern take on creating tableaux. The difference is that the tableau is filmed, with the camera scanning through the scene with close-ups on the various actors/mannequins. There are many examples of these on the internet.
1. Choose an event or situation such as a baseball game.
2. Each person involved will choose a character and an action associated with it. An example would be a hotdog salesperson reaching over someone to give a customer their food.
3. Get into position and freeze. Because this is being filmed people can spread out.
4. Film the whole scene and then zoom in and around the various individuals. The only thing moving should be the camera.
5. Discuss the concept after viewing the video.

Drama Skills:
Building confidence performing in front of people
Developing creativity
Developing facial expression
Developing body language

MASKS (GRADE 4-6)

Masks have a long history of being used in theatre to represent certain characters. When using masks in drama works characters must be portrayed using body language without the aid of facial expressions or voices. Theatre masks have exaggerated features to represent character types such as large angled eyebrows to represent evil.

1. In small groups, students will plan a short drama work using masks. Characters should have specific traits such as evil or kindness. The story can be done as a mime or have a narrator tell the story while the students act it out.
2. Each actor will choose a role to play from their drama work and draw a sketch of what their mask will look like, keeping in mind what parts of the face need to be exaggerated to represent the character.
3. The actors will now create masks with identifiable facial features to help the audience easily identify the character. There are many ways to make masks, some as simple as attaching a picture to a popsicle stick to hold in front of the face, to creating custom made masks to fit the individual student. Patterns can be found on the internet. If there is not time to make masks from scratch blank white masks can be purchased at costume stores which students can decorate to represent their character.
4. Perform drama works for the class.
5. After the performances students can give written or oral feedback regarding the effectiveness of the masks in portraying the character.

Drama Skills:
Drama forms
Developing body language

Working with Masks

DRAMA IDEAS FOR LESSONS BASED ON THE DRAMA CURRICULUM

Making Masks

MIME (GRADE 1-6)

Mime is a style of acting where the actor performs without speaking, instead relying on facial expressions and body language to communicate. Students can therefore focus on developing facial and body expressions without needing to memorize lines or hold scripts. Charades, simple improvs, short or complete drama works can all be done using mime. Begin with simple guided improv in Grade 1 such as, "How can you show me that you're crying?" and develop to short dramas by the end of Grade 6.

Drama Skills:
Developing facial expressions
Developing body language
Drama forms

MINOR TO MAJOR (GRADE 4-6)

Choose a minor character from a story or play such as the footman in *Cinderella*. Write a character sketch for that character and then write a short play where that character becomes the main character. This can be either the same story retold from the characters point of view or can be a new story where reference is made to the original story. For example, if the footman is now the main character he can talk about when he used to work for Cinderella or lived in a castle but now owns his own business as a taxi driver.

Drama Skills:
Character development
Creative process
Developing creativity
Point of view
Retelling stories

MOVE IT (GRADE 1-3)

Students will recreate an occasion or activity from their lives where their bodies are in motion. This can be done individually, in small groups, or as the entire class. Begin with suggestions coming from the teacher.

Some examples of activities that can be performed are:
- community events such as weddings or parades
- things seen in the environment such as birds flying, dogs digging holes, falling leaves, etc.
- customs from other cultures such as dragon dances or communicating with fans;
- life experiences such as winning a baseball game or walking to school the first day.

Drama Skills:
Developing body language
Personal connections to their lives and community

OPPOSITES (GRADE 1 AND 2)

1. Read the book, *Quick as a Cricket* by Audrey Wood, to the class.
2. In pairs, students will choose two animals from the book with opposite traits such as the cricket and snail.
3. Amongst themselves, one student will act out the cricket and the other a snail showing the contrasts of how the two animals move and sound.
4. Keeping the same animals, students will now create different scenarios, real or fictitious, to show how the animals would move. For example, if the snail and cricket were playing basketball, a snail would shuffle slowly to the basketball hoop whereas the cricket would be leaping all over the court.
5. When they are finished, ask for some volunteers to share what they have created.

If you don't have the book *Quick as a Cricket* brainstorm with the class different animals that have opposite character traits and use those for this exercise.

Drama Skills:
Building confidence performing in front of people
Developing creativity

ORCHESTRA (GRADE 4-6)

1. Play a short piece of instrumental music. Discuss how the mood is created and how the dynamics change and why.
2. Divide the class into four groups. Each group will create a piece of music either miming an instrument or using their bodies and voices to create the sound. One student is the conductor of an orchestra. The rest of the students are the musicians. The song will not be an actual melody but a series of sounds.
3. Each person chooses an 'instrument' they will play. As they create their song students will decide when their instrument will be played. The conductor, using his hands, will be in charge of setting the tempo, and creating the dynamics. Perform for the class.

Drama Skills:
Elements of drama
Creating mood

P.I. FOR A DAY (GRADE 4-6)

Students will choose a person at school or home and observe them for a day without being noticed. Students will keep notes regarding how that person walks, talks, dresses, etc. When enough information has been gathered each student will write a short script creating a new character inspired by the observed character traits and habits. The intent is not to write a play based on the observed person but rather to use the observations as a starting point to create a new character. It is not necessary for the class to know who was observed.

Brainstorm appropriate rules for observing someone. This activity is not meant to invade a person's privacy but to develop the art of creating characters based on the observation of the people around us.

Some examples of rules could be:
- don't follow them into the bathroom;
- don't annoy the person by staring at them incessantly;
- don't divulge any personal secrets discovered;
- don't make fun of them when you create your new character.

Practice in the classroom the art of observing discreetly before sending students off to observe people. Students will choose a classmate and have two minutes to walk around the classroom quietly observing them. Who is observing you? Were you caught? Discuss ways to improve the observation process.

Drama Skills:
Character development
Creative process
Developing facial expression
Developing body language

PRESS RELEASE FOR A PLAY (GRADE 4-6)

Ask students to write a press release to announce an upcoming production at the school. The best one can be used in the class newsletter, a parent letter or posted on the school website.

Things that can be included in a press release are:
- the name of the play;
- the date and time of performances;
- the location of the production;
- the admission charge and where tickets can be bought;
- a summary of the play, who some of the actors are (don't use last names if the general public will be reading the release);
- a description of some of the elements of drama used.

Drama Skills:
Elements of drama
Written assignments

PUBLIC SPEAKING (GRADE 4-6)

Public speaking is a skill which will be used throughout life whether it is giving a public thank you, toasting the bride, or delivering a work presentation. In school, students often make presentations for a variety of purposes.

Some of the strategies for effective speeches students can incorporate are to:
- practice beforehand;
- talk at an appropriate volume or if using a microphone, have it close to the mouth;
- speak clearly, enunciate, and at an appropriate speed;
- speak naturally as yourself, without dramatizing the words;
- use cue cards if not able to memorize;
- make eye contact with the audience;
- keep the speech concise and at the required length;
- use visual aids where appropriate.

Drama Skills:
Creating short drama works for specific purposes and audiences
Presentations
Technology

Puppetry (Photo: Jackie Bennett)
Human puppets

PUPPETRY (GRADE 1-6)

Puppets are a way to tell a story with the focus on the puppet and not the actor. Students can either retell a familiar story or create an original drama work. Younger students will do well using finger or hand puppets, and older students will enjoy the challenge of using marionette and shadow puppets or creating their own. Puppet plays are usually told by the actors operating the puppets or by a narrator. Some ideas for using puppets to tell a story are listed below.

- Use ready-made puppets or create puppets to retell a story. Create a small stage with scenery to help compliment the story and to hide the actors if required.
- Attach string to a student's arms so that they are the puppet and have another student act as the puppeteer. The student will move and perform like a puppet while the story is told.
- Make 2D puppets with straws and grommets to move the limbs. On an overhead move the puppet so that it shows on the wall.

Drama Skills:
Drama forms
Retelling stories
Developing facial and vocal expression
Creative process

PUT YOURSELF IN HIS SHOES (GRADE 4-6)
You have probably heard the expression, "Walk a mile in his shoes." This expression is particularly appropriate for acting. Spending time with someone similar to your character helps you to experience what it is like to be them. It can also encourage empathy for others.
1. Students will choose a person from their lives, or someone they have read about that has experienced something they have not. For example, being in the hospital, needing to walk five miles to get water, or switching schools mid-year.
2. They will write a paragraph describing the event and how the people involved might be feeling.
3. Students will then write a short monologue placing themselves in that situation, using their reflections to show empathy.
4. The monologue will be performed in a costume that complements the situation.

Drama Skills:
Character development
Point of view

RADIO PLAYS (GRADE 4-6)
In the days before television, traditional radio plays relied on vocal expression, sound effects, and music to tell a story.
1. Play a recorded radio play for the class. (These can be found on the internet.)
2. Discuss the elements that comprise a radio play and what makes it different from a stage play or television show.
3. In small groups, students will choose a well-known story to rewrite as a short script. The script will include dialogue and sound and music cues. Students can add commercials or public announcements if they want.
4. Practice the play and when ready, record it.
5. Play back the recording to hear if any changes need to be made. If editing software is available, make corrections; otherwise, it may be necessary to rerecord the play.
6. When completed, play for the class.

Drama Skills:
Drama forms
Creating short drama works for specific purposes and audiences
Developing vocal expression
Retelling stories

READ AND PREDICT (GRADE 1-3)
Read out loud a story that has a surprise ending and that the class is not familiar with. Stop at a critical point and have students continue the story by improvising in character what they predict will happen next. Afterwards read the story all the way through to see how accurate their predictions were.

Drama Skills:
Developing creativity
Predictions

READER'S THEATRE (GRADE 4-6)
Reader's theatre is where a story is read out loud using vocal expression to represent the different characters, emotion, and mood. Usually, it is performed by one actor without the use of costumes or props. Students will choose a well-known story and shorten it to keep within an assigned time frame. After practicing on their own they will read it to the class or a younger audience.

Drama Skills:
Retelling stories
Developing vocal expression

REAL OR NOT REAL (GRADE 1)
1. With the class, make a list of characters found in different stories, and place them in the following categories: real, fictitious that could be real, and not found in real life.
   Examples of the three types of characters are:
   A real character: Jane Goodall from *The Watcher: Jane Goodall's Life with the Chimps* by Jeanette Winter.
   A fictitious character that could be real: David from *David Gets in Trouble* by David Shannon.
   Characters not found in real life: The Grinch from *How the Grinch Stole Christmas!* by Dr. Seuss.
2. Discuss the differences between the three categories and how they relate to real life.

Drama Skills:
Reality versus fiction
Character development
Personal connections to their lives and community

RECAP (GRADE 1-3)
1. Read a short story to the class.
2. Choose an individual or small group to stand up and retell the story by acting it out in one minute or less. To give everyone the opportunity to perform this can be done over several days, each time a new story is read to the class.
   Extension:
   1. Read a story that is not familiar to the class.
   2. In small groups, students will retell and perform the same story using a dramatic form of their choice. i.e. skit, dance, puppets, tableaus, slide show, interviews, point of view, etc.

Drama Skills:
Building confidence performing in front of people
Drama forms
Retelling stories

REPURPOSE IT (GRADE 3-4)
Give students an object and ask them to find another way it can realistically be used and show it being used as a prop in a short drama. For example, a spoon could be used as a spade; a shoe could be used as a fly swatter; a book can be used as a weight; or a pencil can be used as a tongue depressor.

Drama Skills:
Developing creativity
Improvisation

ROCK STAR (GRADE 4)
Divide the class into six groups and assign a rock form, sedimentary, metamorphic, or igneous to each group. Each group will create short skits where someone is interviewing a rock star and their band. The music groups are based on the rock form they were assigned. Students can wear costumes and perform music as well as answer questions about themselves during the interview. Details shared should be related to their rock form.

An example would be the band called Sedimentary Flat Rock or SFR for short. During the interview, we find out things such as they like to hang around the beach when they're not performing, and their favourite colour is grey.

Drama Skills:
Creating short drama works for specific purposes

ROLE PLAYING (GRADE 1-6)
Drama provides a safe environment to explore social and personal issues and help students find solutions for conflicts. By being in character, students can sometimes say things they wouldn't normally feel comfortable talking about in front of their peers. It may also be more effective for students to see these issues played out rather than to have the teacher teach about them.

As not all problems can be solved in a short amount of time role playing will not necessarily give solutions for the issue being explored. Sometimes it will merely provide students with the opportunity to see other points of view and to express their ideas and concerns.

Role playing, usually done through improvised activities rather than scripted ones, has the following benefits:
- it allows students to be someone else even if it is someone who is nothing like them;
- it helps students to express how they feel about issues they are trying to deal with;
- it allows students to see other points of view and leads to a better understanding of others;
- it helps students to look for positive and constructive ways to problem solve.

For a more in depth look at teaching role playing refer to Chapter Eight.

Drama Skills:
Role Play: exploring solutions to everyday problems and social issues

RUNWAY (GRADE 1-3)
Create a space that can be used as a fashion runway with a bin of costumes and accessories at one end. Students, one at a time, will go to the bin, put on the first costume or accessory they touch, and then walk down the runway as a character represented by that outfit. For example, if rabbit ears are selected the student would hop down the runway. Once students reach the end of the runway, they will strike a pose in role and then turn around and go back up the aisle. As the person is walking down the runaway, the next student is getting into costume to begin their walk.

For Grade 4-6: The next step is for students to create a costume for a character from a dramatic work and then have a fashion show with each student walking the runway in role. At the end of the runway, they pose in character and say one statement about their character. For example, "I am an important ruler in my kingdom."

Drama Skills:
Building confidence performing in front of people
Character development
Costumes

SAME THING FOUR WAYS (GRADE 3-6)
In small groups use each of the arts strands (music, dance, art, and drama) to retell a story four different ways. Fr example, poster, song, skit, dance.

Drama Skills:
Retelling stories

SET (GRADE 4-5)
Students will make miniature stages with set pieces, scenery, and props to establish time and setting for a play being studied or one that they have written. Shoeboxes or cereal boxes are ideal to use for the stage. Sets should be designed to portray the overall theme of the play. After stages have been created students will make a presentation explaining their choices.

Drama Skills:
Elements of drama

SHOPPING SPREE (GRADE 1-3)
Divide the class into small groups. One person will play the shop owner, and the other members of the group will be shoppers. They will improvise a shopping experience at a store of their choice. To make a link to math, the improv will end with a money transaction that involves giving change. For example, a student decides to buy a stuffed animal. The cost is $1.75 but she only has a $1.70. She asks her friends to lend her the extra 5 cents. The friend hands over a quarter resulting in 20 cents in change.

Drama skills:
Developing creativity and playwriting
Improvisation

SHOW ME (GRADE 1-2)
While the class is moving around the room call out various activities and skills students may experience at school or home. The students will start acting out what you have said until you call out another action. For example: "Show me what you look like when you're skating." Students will skate around the room. "Show me what you look like when you're listening well." Students will sit down where they are with hands on their laps. Use as many examples as time will allow.

Drama skills:
Building confidence performing in front of people
Personal connections to their lives and community

SMILE/FROWN (GRADE 1-3)
The objective of this exercise is to help students develop the ability to offer sensitive peer feedback.
1. Gather a box of items from outside the classroom that are in various conditions. For example, a picture of a dog, an old teddy bear, or a half-eaten sandwich.
2. With the class brainstorm examples of feedback that would make someone smile and examples of feedback that would make them frown.
3. Hold up each of the items one at a time. In pairs, students will give feedback that will give a smile and give a frown to each thing. For example, if the object is a picture of a large dog a smile could be, "It looks like he would be a good guard dog." A frown would be, "The dog looks like the ugliest dog in the world."
4. Students will share some of their answers. Discuss how they would feel if they received negative feedback and ways they can give responses that are constructive without causing hurt feelings to others.
5. The next step is to give constructive criticism about the items in the box in a sensitive way. This can include an assessment of the article, feelings associated with it, or ways to improve it.

Drama Skills:
Analyze, reflect, respond
Peer critiquing

SOUNDSCAPE (GRADE 1-6)
A soundscape is recreating an event or situation by using only sound effects. The most effective ones have a story that builds to a climax and returns to the mood of the beginning.

Begin with teaching the class a soundscape that has already been created. One of my favourites is "making rain," a quick one to teach students before they create their own. See Chapter Twelve for a detailed description of how to do this. Other examples of soundscapes can be found on YouTube.

Put the students into smaller groups to make their own soundscapes.
Some ideas of events that can be used to make a soundscape are:
- thunderstorms
- canoe trip
- a noisy classroom
- roller coaster ride
- watching a scary movie

Drama Skills:
Creating short drama works for specific purposes and audiences
Drama forms

SPEECHES (GRADE 4-6)
1. Students will pick someone from the time period they are studying in social studies. This can either be a real person such as Laura Secord or a person in an occupation such as a blacksmith from pioneer times.
2. After researching the person or occupation, students will write a short speech in that person's voice. The speech can be written for a specific event such as King Arthur addressing his knights at the round table or in a casual setting where an athlete from ancient Greece is telling his family about his race.
3. Wearing appropriate clothing, students will present their speech to the class. Props may also be used.

A lesson plan that involves using speeches for political presentations can be found in Chapter Twelve.

Drama Skills:
Performing

STAGED READING (GRADE 4-6)
If you don't have time to put on an entire play, consider having a staged reading where actors read their parts from a stage. Rehearsals are still held but require only a few weeks as opposed to several months. A representation of props, costumes, and lighting can be used.
Staged readings can be done in a variety of ways. Following is one of these ways.
1. The cast will sit in rows facing the audience.
2. At the beginning of each scene, only the characters in that scene will stand up and move to the front of the performance area. Actors will read from their script that they can either hold or place on a music stand in front of them. Actors remain standing and in character for the whole scene.
3. At the end of the scene, all actors will sit down, even if they are in the next one. This helps the audience to know the scene is over. A person can also hold large cards to announce which scene is next.
4. Continue steps two and three until the play is done. If there is more than one act take a break with an intermission.

Rehearsals are essential for a staged reading so that the actors are familiar with their lines, have developed their acting, and know their cues.

Drama skills:
Building confidence performing in front of people
Presenting
Developing vocal and facial expression
Focus/stay in role

STORYBOARDS (GRADE 4-6)
A storyboard is a series of blank squares on a large piece of paper where each scene of a drama work is described, either using point form or illustrations. This is a tool used to help organize creative thoughts before working on the first draft.

Drama Skills:
Develop creativity

STORYTELLING (GRADE 3-6)
Storytelling is the art of telling a memorized story to an audience using facial expressions, voices, gestures, dynamics and tempo to help with the interpretation of the story. Storytelling develops the ability to speak clearly and expressively.

Students will pick a fairy tale, fable, or favourite picture book.

1. They will write the fairy tale in their own words and practice reading it to make sure it is within the assigned time limit.
2. As part of the creative process, students will need class time to write their stories and to perform for partners in order to benefit from peer and teacher editing.
3. The story can be memorized or written on cue cards in point form. If cue cards are used, they are meant for reminders not to read the entire story from. Hint: Students should number the cards, so if they drop them, they can quickly be put back in order.
4. Some of the things students should utilize while telling their story are to use the voice or body to create sound effects, use different voices for characters when they speak, use exaggeration and facial expressions, and engage with the audience.
5. When ready, stories will be performed for the class. You won't have time for all the students to perform in one lesson. You can either spill over into several lessons or have a schedule where two people a day will perform until all are completed. You can draw names from a hat, so everyone needs to be prepared to give everyone a fair advantage.
6. If all classes in the junior division are doing storytelling, consider taking the top two or three from each class to perform for the school or parents.

Drama Skills:
Building confidence performing in front of people
Creating short drama works for specific purposes and audiences
Developing vocal expression
Drama forms
Retelling stories

SURVEY SAYS (GRADE 1-6)
Collect data on any subject by conducting a survey. Analyze the data. Students will then present the findings in the form of a newscast. For primary grades the newscast will be performed live, using guest speakers if they wish. Junior grades can perform live or film the newscast, with segments showing the survey process.

Drama Skills:
drama forms
presenting

SWITCH (GRADE 1-3)

Individually, students will improvise a situation where there can be two different points of view. Either the teacher or students will give the actor a situation such as a young person wanting to stay up late on a school night. The improv will start off showing one character's point of view (child wants to stay up to watch the lunar eclipse) and when the teacher says "switch," change to the other person's point of view (parent wants the child to get a good night's sleep because it's a school night). The actor will go back and forth until the teacher feels they have represented both points of view. Allow around one minute per student.

Drama Skills:
Character development
Point of view

SYMBOLISM (GRADE 6)

Symbols are used in various forms to represent meaning without words. Students will begin by making a list of symbols found around the school and well-known ones from outside school, such as red equals stop and the skull and cross bones indicating poison. From there they will expand to identifying symbols used in plays, either one that they have recently attended or a script they are studying.

Examples of symbols used in theatre are:
Gestures: *A finger to the lip means silence, or fingers in a V means peace*
Props: *Ripped up flowers means anger, or a suitcase means travel*
Expression: *Eyes closed means fear, or mouth open means astonishment*
Costume: *Black clothing means grieving, or evil*
Setting: *Old ripped furniture means poverty, or abandonment*

Post five construction sheets on the wall for each of the five areas listed above. Students will write or draw pictures of symbols they have seen in a drama work on the appropriate sheet.
Extension: Create a short drama work using several of the symbols found by students.

Drama Skills:
Symbols

TABLEAUX (GRADE 1-6)

A tableau is a picture that is created by a group of people frozen in position while depicting a scene. For example, three people are staring up at a fourth person pretending to be a tree. Those four people remain frozen without speaking for a pre-arranged count of time.

Tableaux are usually presented with a series of scenes, moving smoothly from one to the next. Tableaux can be used in all areas of the curriculum where students need to describe or explain specific expectations. For example, they can be used in social studies when students are describing the different jobs that people do in a pioneer village.

To begin, have the students make one tableau at a time so that they can learn the technique.

1. Divide the class into four. Provide a different scene for each group that would involve lots of people, such as a baseball game.
2. Each group will create a tableau while the rest of the class observes. One person starts the tableau off by freezing in position as a character from the assigned scene. In the case of the baseball game, they would stand in the middle ready to swing an imaginary bat. The rest of the students from the group will join the scene, interacting appropriately with the others already in the scene. For example, students could be the other players, umpires, the crowd watching the game, or a hot dog seller. When all members of the group are in the scene, they will freeze creating the tableau.
3. Proceed with the next group until all groups have performed.
4. The next step is to divide the class into small groups. Each group will choose a scene and decide who will be which character. They will have a brief practice and then perform them for the class.

Once the class is comfortable, you can begin to tell stories using tableaux. This can be done in various ways.

Grade 1-3
Events
- Students can describe an event using three or four tableaux. For example, at an amusement park, the first tableau could be waiting in line for their turn on the roller coaster, the second would be sitting in their seats eager to proceed, the third screaming as the car goes down the track, and the forth waiting in line again. Students should attempt to make each character in the scene different. For example, one person on the roller coaster could be screaming, one about to throw up, and another with their eyes closed.

Grade 4-6
PowerPoint or slide show
- Students can create a PowerPoint presentation or slide show using a series of tableaux. One or two students will be the presenters and the other students in the group will be the PowerPoint images. The speaker does what would happen in a real presentation, start to talk about a subject, and then clicks the button to move to the next image.

For example, if the presentation is about climate conditions in the North Pole, the presenter might say, "In the winter a favourite activity of young people in the North Pole is to make snowmen. Click." At click, the students not presenting quickly get into a tableau showing young people making a snowman. They remain frozen until 'click' is said again and then they move into the next tableau depicting what has been said. This drama work can be done scripted or improvised.

Storytelling
Students in small groups will pick or write a short story. Someone will tell or read the story while the rest of the group become the illustrations using tableaux. The narrator can signal the next tableau by saying, 'page turn' or by designating the changes during practice.

Silent Story

Using the creative process, students in small groups will write a short story that has no dialogue and contains lots of imagery. Using tableaux, they will tell the story without a narrator. The final step is to select a piece of appropriate music to accompany the story. After sufficient practice, the stories will be performed.

Drama Skills:
Building confidence performing in front of people
Drama forms
Developing facial and body expression
Retelling stories

Tableaux (Photo: Jackie Bennett)
Roller coaster

Tableaux (Photo: Jackie Bennett)
Baseball game

TAKE A MINUTE (GRADE 4-6)

Create a one-minute drama based on an event that shows tension. Set a timer. A student will improvise the scene until the timer goes off. Props or sound effects can be used but are not necessary.

An example would be a student who has been sent to the principal's office and is waiting to be seen. The scene can be set by the student pacing back and forth in the hall, clock ticking loudly, student muttering about why they are worried, student silent and miserable or anything else to show that it is a long, stressful minute.

Other ideas for a one-minute drama could be waiting to eat pizza, waiting to open a birthday present, waiting for parents to wake up so you can go camping or the last minute of a basketball game.

Drama Skills:
Creating short drama works for specific purpose or audience
Elements of drama: tension

THIS IS NOT A DRILL (GRADE 1-6)
There are many real-life situations or events where students need to be prepared to respond appropriately. Following are ideas for improvisation or written scripts students can perform to practice various types of emergencies or stressful situations.
- Students will improvise or plan short skits to demonstrate how to deal with safety and emergency situations at school such as stranger danger, fire drills, and bus safety.
- Create short drama works to show new situations that might cause anxiety for students such as going to the dentist, first day of hockey, or a new babysitter.
- Write a short skit based on a make-believe situation such as your hamster is moving to Mars or it's raining eggs.

- Newscasts, safety videos, posters, etc. are other forms students can use for this exercise.

Drama Skills:
Creating short dramas for a specific purpose or audience
Personal connections to their lives and communities

THOUGHT TRACKING (GRADE 4-6)

Thought tracking is an exercise used to answer questions about a scene or character. As students perform their drama works, tap a student on the shoulder. The scene would stop, with students staying where they are. Either have a prearranged question such as, "When you are tapped you will tell me why your character is behaving the way they are," or ask a question that is relevant to what is happening at that moment. When the answer is given, continue the scene.

Drama Skills:
Character development
Creative process

TWO SIDES OF THE COIN (GRADE 4-6)

Read a book or books to the class showing two distinct sides of the same story, such as *Jack and the Beanstalk* and *The Beanstalk Incident* by Tim Paulson. Discuss the two sides of the story.

Divide students into groups of six to eight. Each group will choose a well-known story. Half of each group will create a short skit telling the story from the main character's point of view, and the other half will create a short skit telling the story from another character's point of view. For example, the tale *Cinderella*. One skit could be from Cinderella's point of view, and the other skit could be from the stepmother's point of view. The two groups will work on their own version without seeing what the other half is doing so they are not influenced by the other point of view.

After all the stories have been presented, each group as a whole will create a new skit that shows how the characters have changed their point of view based on what they heard. For example, Cinderella might say she didn't know her stepmother wanted to avoid her because she was missing Cinderella's father.

Drama Skills:
Character development
Elements of Drama: role/character
Point of view
Retelling stories

TWO STARS AND A WISH (GRADE 1-3)

"Two stars and a wish" is used in many schools as a quick way for students to evaluate their or another's work. A student, when offering feedback, will state two positive things and one area to be improved. This can be a general response to an overall work or an answer to a specific question such as, "What is your response to the costumes that were used?"

Drama Skills:
Analyze, reflect, respond
Peer critiquing

USE YOUR WORDS (GRADE 2-3)
Students will create short drama works where the main focus of the script is on the dialogue. See Chapter Twelve for a detailed lesson plan for two exercises, David's drama and cell phone dramas, that rely on words to create a scene.

Drama Skills:
Creating short drama works

USING DRAMA SKILLS FOR A PURPOSE (GRADE 1-6)
All skills need to be used as they are developing. Basketball drills are used during a game. Learning how to play notes on an instrument leads to a concert. The same goes for learning drama skills. Drama is not just acting on stage or role playing. There are numerous occasions throughout the year where drama skills can be used to prepare short drama works for a specific purpose.

Some examples would be:
- short plays about peace during a Remembrance Day ceremony;
- skits for assemblies celebrating character traits such as respect and perseverance;
- skits about first day jitters to be performed for kindergarten students;
- mask works for a Halloween assembly;
- short radio plays to be heard over the school PA system;
- public speaking and storytelling.

Drama Skills:
Creating short drama works for specific purposes and audience
Developing creativity

VOICES IN THE HEAD (GRADE 4-6)
This is an improv exercise for making decisions when right and wrong are clearly indicated.
1. Students will get into groups of three and form a line.
2. The person in the middle will state a dilemma such as, "Should I take my sister's cupcake?"
3. The other two students will stand on each side of the middle student to represent right and wrong.
4. As the outer students offer their opinions on what to do based on right and wrong, the middle student will mime whatever they say.
5. Continue the scene until the person with the dilemma tells the other two people to stop telling him what to do and makes his decision.

An example would be as follows:
Actor
Should I take my sister's cupcake?
Right
Walk away from the cupcake. (Actor walks away.)
Wrong
No, don't walk away. Grab the cupcake and lick it, so no one else wants it. (Actor does as told.)
Right
But that's wrong. Run in circles until you forget about the cupcake. (Actor runs in circles.)
Actor
Stop telling me what to do. I have decided not to take my sister's cupcake.

Drama Skills:
Point of view

WARM-UP EXERCISES (GRADE 1-6)
Exercises to warm up the voice and body are useful for not only preparing the body for performing but to also help students focus before a performance. There are many available. Here are a few examples to get you started.

Face stretch/ scrunch:
Stretch the entire face as far as possible, including opening the mouth and eyelids and then make them as tight and small as possible. Repeat.

Irritated horse:
After taking a deep breath, let the air out noisily through the mouth, causing the lips to vibrate, and therefore making a sound like an irritated horse.

Hold the breath:
Take a deep breath in from the diaphragm and hold as long as possible. This should be done silently and without the shoulders moving. Students like it when you make it a competition to see who can hold their breath the longest. Have everyone breathe in at the same time, and when they need to take in another breath, they sit down. Last person standing wins.

Blow bubbles:
Take a deep breath and when you blow out pretend you are making a giant bubble.

Hut!:
Bend over as if in a football huddle and yell "hut" repeatedly, letting the air come out sharply with each hut, feeling the diaphragm moving.

Drama Skills:
Preparing for performances

WAX MUSEUM (GRADE 1-6)

1. Pick a subject from a curriculum area where different types of people are found, such as medieval or pioneer times.
2. Divide the class into groups of five or six.
3. Each student within the group will become an expert on a different person found within that area of study. For example, students in Grade 1 learning about their community could be a bus driver, neighbour, store owner, librarian, and police officer.
4. Once research has been completed, each person will choose five things about their character to share.
5. The group will stand in a row at the front of the class dressed as the person they are representing. They will pose in character and freeze like a wax figure until it is their turn to present. When they present, they will step forward, tell their five key things, and then freeze again as the next person presents.
6. When all the people in the group are finished, they stop being wax figures and answer any questions the rest of the class might have about their characters.

Drama Skills:
Character development
Presenting
Focus/ stay in role
Personal connections to their lives and community
Personal connections to life in the past

WHAT HAPPENS NEXT? (GRADE 1-6)

The teacher or students will provide a premise for a scenario such as, "You are sneaking into a dark house after your curfew and the lights suddenly come on." Students will improvise what happens next.

Drama Skills:
Developing creativity

WHAT SHOULD I WEAR? (GRADE 1-2)

1. Brainstorm items of clothing or accessories you would use for the different seasons. For example, a scarf, swimsuit, and snowshoes.
2. Write these items on separate pieces of paper and put in a container.
3. Brainstorm activities people do in the different seasons. For example, skiing or playing in the leaves. Write these each on separate pieces of paper and put them in a different box. For younger students put a picture above each word.
4. A volunteer draws out a piece of paper from each box without reading them out loud. They perform a ten-second mime that uses both words.
5. The audience will make guesses as well as suggesting what the appropriate clothing would be for the activity performed. Whoever guesses correctly will take the next turn.
An example of this would be if one card one says "bathing suit" and the second card says "skating," the student will mime putting on a bathing suit and then skating. A correct guess would be a variation of, "You are skating with your bathing suit on."

Drama Skills:
Building self-confidence performing in front of people
Personal connections to their lives and community

WHAT SHOULD YOU DO? (GRADE 1-3)

This exercise helps students develop problem-solving skills. The teacher or students will state a problem and ask the actors, "What should you do?" The students will improvise potential solutions. Start by doing this with the whole class performing and then allow one or two students to perform at a time.

Example of problems to present to the class are:
- You can't find your reading bag. What should you do?
- Someone wants your lunch. What should you do?
- Your underwear keeps falling down. What should you do?

Drama Skills:
Developing creativity
Problem-solving

WHAT WOULD HAPPEN? (GRADE 4-6)

Ask questions that are geared to help students think outside the box. Students will write a one-minute play based on their answers.

Examples of questions:
- What would happen if all the birds in the sky were blue?
- What would happen if everyone wore skates to school?
- What would happen if when the teacher spoke, bubbles came out of their ears?
- What would happen if all the chickens ran away?

Drama Skills:
Developing creativity

WHAT WOULD IT BE LIKE? (GRADE 1-3)

Students will create and perform short drama works about something they've always wanted to do, or would never want to do, so that they can experience what it would be like. Some examples would be getting a new puppy, going to a new school, learning to be a magician or flying to the moon.

Drama Skills:
Developing creativity

WHAT WOULD WE LOOK LIKE? (GRADE 1-3)

1. Suggest a situation such as, "What would we look like if it started snowing in July?" Students will strike a pose to illustrate their reaction to the question. Select a few students who demonstrated strong facial and body language to share their poses with the class.
2. Each student will think of their own situation and share it with the class. When they are in their pose, take a picture.
3. Give a copy of each student's pose to them to use as an illustration for a short story they will write about the situation they chose.

Drama Skills:
Building confidence performing for people
Developing facial expressions
Developing body language

WHAT YOU IMAGINE AND WHAT YOU KNOW (GRADE 4-6)
1. In small groups, students will choose a person, real or fictitious, from a period being studied. They will brainstorm what they think that person was like including their gestures, costumes, job description, and lifestyle.
2. The groups will each create a short drama work about their characters.
3. After all the drama works have been performed students will research facts about their character and the time they lived in. Students will make adjustments to their drama work to make it historically correct based on what they now know.
4. The new version of the drama works will be performed.
5. Students will reflect on the process and make observations. They will answer questions such as, "How does your drama work change after learning about the period and why does that matter?"

Although this is best suited for junior grades, a simpler version can be modified for Grade 1-3.

Drama Skills:
Analyze, reflect, respond
Presenting
Creating short drama works for specific purpose or audience
Creative process
Developing creativity

WHAT'S THE DIFFERENCE? (GRADE 4-6)
1. Divide the students into small groups and assign a different drama form to each group. The groups will become experts in their area and make a presentation to the class.
2. After all the presentations have been done students will write a short report showing the difference between the form they presented, and a form presented by another group.
3. In the same groups, students will create and present a short drama work. This drama work will be performed two times, once using the original drama form they researched and the second time using the form they used for comparison.
4. Students will follow up with another short report to reflect on the process of creating the same work with two different forms.

Some examples of different forms and their elements are:

Street performers
- Performances are shorter due to the length of time the audience will stay to watch.
- The audience is close to the performer.
- Microphones and speakers may be used to be heard over traffic.
- Minimal costumes and props are used.

Live theatre
- The performance area has a stage, curtains, and lights.
- The script is performed in chronological order.
- Actors use exaggerated gestures so people at the back can see them.

Puppet shows
- The audience is close to the action.
- There is limited space for movement.

Movies
- Actors can be clearly seen and heard.
- The story is filmed out of sequence.
- Scenes can be filmed in unlimited locations.

TV sitcoms
- They often have an audience while taping.
- Because of space limitations scenes occur in fewer locations.

Circus
- There is less talking and more performing.
- Music is used to provide tension.
- Performers often use mime with exaggerated movement.

Drama Skills:
Analyze, reflect and respond
Drama forms
Presentations

WHAT'S THE SENSE? (GRADE 1-3)

1. Students will demonstrate how their character is feeling and what they are smelling, hearing, seeing, and tasting during a short drama work.
2. In groups of five, students will choose an occasion such as Thanksgiving. Each student will write a sentence using one of the senses. For example, Student One could say that Thanksgiving feels like hugs from Grandma, Student Two can say Thanksgiving smells like roast turkey etc.
3. Their five sentences will be written on a large piece of paper and illustrated by the group.
4. The group will then present their senses to the class. A person will read his own sentence while the rest of the group illustrates the sentence by creating a tableau. He then joins the group to be in the next tableau as the next person steps out from the group to read their line. Repeat this until all sentences have been read.

Drama Skills:
Presenting
Developing creativity
Developing body language
Personal connections to their lives and community

WHAT'S YOUR PROBLEM? (GRADE 1-3)
Students will create short skits or improvisations that show a mathematical problem.

An example of this would be a situation where there are not enough chairs. Two students are each sitting on a chair. Two more students enter but there are no more chairs. The characters in the skit discuss, using math equations, what could be done so that everyone can have a seat. They could say things like, there are two chairs, but we need two more which means we need four chairs. Or, if we took away the two chairs, there would be none so everyone would be without a chair.

Drama Skills:
Developing creativity
Problem-solving

WHERE ARE WE? (GRADE 1-3)
Using words that focus on each of the senses the teacher will describe a setting. Students, with their eyes closed, will visualize what is being said. After each description, a few people can guess where they think they are. If no one guesses correctly, the teacher will continue repeating the previous statements and adding a new one until someone guesses where they are.

An example of this would be:

Leader: It is smelly. Where are we?
A student: In the bathroom?
Leader: That's not where we are. It is smelly, and I don't hear any cars. Where are we?
A student: Are we at the dump?
Leader: That's not where we are. It is smelly, I don't hear any cars, and I feel prickly hay with my feet. Where are we?
A student: Are we at a farm?
Leader: Close. It is smelly, I don't hear any cars, I feel prickly hay with my feet, and I hear oinking. Where are we?
A student: Are we in a pig pen?
Leader: Yes.

Drama Skills:
Developing creativity

WHERE IS THE AUDIENCE? (GRADE 1-6)
It is useful for young actors when practicing their drama works to be aware of where the audience will be. This will aid students with blocking and remind them not to have their backs to the audience while performing. It is therefore helpful to have students draw a mural of people sitting in their seats that can be posted in the practice space to represent the audience. Or, each student can draw or paint a self-portrait of their head and shoulders which can be cut out to make a collage to represent an audience. Every time students practice their drama works, they can perform facing the mural.

Drama Skills:
Blocking
Developing acting skills

Where is the Audience?
Mural

WHO AM I? (GRADE 1-3)

Brainstorm with the class a list of jobs people have in the community. Write each one on a separate piece of paper and put in a container. Students will select one and then do a short improvisation without saying the name of the profession.

For example, if they are playing the part of a bus driver, they cannot use the word bus or driver. Instead, they can say things such as, "I want you to come on quietly, no pushing. Only two people on each seat. No standing when we're moving."

Students will guess the profession. If they are correct, they will be next to perform.

Drama Skills:
Personal connections to their lives and communities

WHO IS THIS FOR? (GRADE 4-6)

1. Brainstorm with the class different people you could tell a story to. For example, a toddler, parent, police officer, friend, bus driver etc. Write each of these in large letters on an eight by ten piece of paper.
2. Discuss with the class what might change in the delivery of the story depending on who the story is being told to.
3. Students will choose a nursery rhyme they have memorized. As they recite it, hold up the various papers, one at a time, for the actor to see. The actor will continue to tell the nursery rhyme but change their delivery based on which person is on the paper. The way the words are spoken, facial expressions, gestures, tempos, etc., need to change according to who the audience is.

Drama Skills:
Creating short drama works for specific purposes and audience
Developing vocal expression
Performing

WHO IS YOUR AUDIENCE? (GRADE 4-6)
Brainstorm with the class how and why different audiences might respond differently to a product. Students will create commercials for a product but will adapt it according to the audience that is being targeted. Flashcards with different age groups on it such as child, teen, parent, and senior will indicate how the student delivers the commercial.

For a more detailed instruction on how to teach this activity, please refer to Chapter Twelve.

Drama Skills:
Creating short drama works for specific purposes and audience
Point of view

WHO OWNS THIS? (GRADE 1)
Have a collection of objects or large photos of objects—things such as a pair of skates, lunch box, or a paint brush. As a class, students will look at each object and decide who would own it. They would then move according to how that person would use it.

The next step is to use that object, acting like someone who would not typically use it. For example, if you had a soother, you would pretend to be a baby using it the first time. The second time you might be a teacher sucking on a soother while teaching math.

Invite individuals to share with the class their ideas.

Drama Skills:
Developing creativity

WHOSE SEAT IS IT? (GRADE 1-3)
1. Make a list of different types of seats and write them onto separate cards.
2. Place a single chair in the centre of the stage area.
3. A student will draw a card and perform a one-minute improvisation without saying what type of seat they are on. At the end of the minute, the class will guess "whose seat is it?" Whoever guesses correctly will be the next person to perform.

Some examples of seats are a roller coaster, church pew, a bench next to a baby who needs a diaper changer, the back seat of a car during a bumpy ride, or a bean bag.

Drama Skills:
Developing creativity

WHY DID YOU DO THAT? (GRADE 4-6)
An actor will play the part of a therapist or doctor. The doctor will interview, as part of a TV show, a villain from a play or story. Questions and answers should have an emphasis on exploring why characters may do the things that they do. These questions and answers can be pre-planned or improvised.

Examples of questions that could be asked are:
- Mr. Wolf, why did you feel the need to blow down the pig's houses?
- Mr. Wolf, did you ever wonder how the pigs feel when you threaten them?
- Jack, what made you decide to break into the giant's castle?

Drama Skills:
Character development
Point of view

WORDS, FACE, BODY (GRADE 1-3)

This is a quick exercise to show how the same thing can be expressed in three ways, by using words, facial expressions, and body language.

The teacher will give a situation to the class such as being excited to go to the aquarium. When he says "words," the class will improv using only words to show their excitement. After fifteen seconds he will say "face." The class then shows their excitement on their faces only, and then fifteen seconds later when he says "body" the class does the same thing using their bodies. Repeat a few times with different situations. Students should be careful to only use the form of expression given.

When this has been mastered, invite three students to the performing area. Assign each student one of the forms of expression. Give a situation. For 30 seconds, each of the three students will act out the situation using their category only. You will, therefore, have three students showing the same situation in three different ways.

Drama Skills:
Developing vocal and facial expression
Developing body language

INDEX

LEARNING SKILLS AND CORRESPONDING ACTIVITIES:
Analyze, Reflect, Respond
Change the mood (Grade 3-6) / In and Out (4-6) / Record performance (4-6) / Smile/frown (1-3) Two stars and a wish (1-3) / What you imagine and what you know (4-6) / What's the difference? (4-6)

Blocking
Where is the audience (Grade 1-6)

Building Confidence Performing in Front of People
Animal crackers (K- Grade 1) / Art Gallery (3-6) / Audition improvisation (1-6) / Change (1-3) Change the mood 2 (1-3) / Character, place, and me (4-6) / Choral reading (1-6) / Dynamics (1) Fake it till you make it (4-6) / For real (1-3) / Guided imagery (K-1) / Mannequin challenge (1-6) Opposites (1 and 2) Recap (1-3) / Runway (1-3) / Show me (1-2) / Staged reading (4-6) / Tableaux (1-6) What should I wear? (1-2) / What would we look like? (1-3)

Character Development
A day in the life of (Grade 1-3) / Act your age (4-6) / Character development (1-6) / Character on the wall 1-6) / Character sketch (4-6) / Five things to know about me (1-6) / Minor to major (4-6) / P.I. for a day (4-6) Put yourself in his shoes (4-6) / Real or not real (1) / Runway (1-3) / Two sides of the coin (4-6) / Switch (1-3) / Thought tracking (4-6) / Wax museum (1-6) / Why did you do that? (4-6)

Costumes
Art Gallery (Grade 3-6) / Runway (1-3)

Creating and Presenting Short Drama Works for Specific Purposes and Audience
Art Gallery (Grade 4-6) / Back and forth (4- 6) / Change the mood (3-6) / Commercials (1-6) / Cultural celebrations (1-6) / Drama jobs (5) / Interviews/ talk shows (4-6) / Judge Judy (5-6) /Point of view (1-6) Public speaking (4-6) / Radio plays (4-6) / Rock Star (4) / Soundscape (1-6) / Speeches (4-6) / Staged reading (4-6) / Storytelling (3-6) / Take a minute (4-6) / This Is Not a Drill (1-6) / Use Your Words (2-3) / Using drama skills for a purpose (1-6) / Wax museum (1-6) / We need someone else (2-3) / What's the difference (4-6) What's the sense? (1-3) / What you imagine and what you know (4-6) / Who is this for? (4-6) Who is your audience? (4-6)

Creating Moods
Gymnastic ribbons (K- Grade 4) / In the mood (1-3) / Orchestra (4-6)

Creative process
Drama journals (Grade 4-6) / P.I. for a day (4-6) / Puppetry (1-6) / Radio plays (4-6) / Thought tracking (4-6) / What you imagine and what you know (4-6)

Cultural Representation
Cultural celebrations (Grade 1-6)

Developing Acting and Performing Skills
Fake it till you make it (4-6) / Where is the audience? (1-6)

Developing Body Language
Change the mood 2 (1-3) / Escalate (2-6) / Greek theatre (5) / Gymnastic ribbons (K-4) / How can you show? (1-3) / Laryngitis (1-3) / Mannequin challenge (1-6) / Masks (4-6) / Mime (1-6) / Move it (1-3) / P.I. for a day (4-6) / Pick a character (4-6) / Shopping spree (1-3) / Tableaux (1-6) / What did you say? (4-6) What would we look like? (1-3) / What's the sense? (1-3) / Words, body, face (1-3)

Developing Creativity and Playwriting
Advice hall (Grade 1- 6) / And then this happened... (1-3) / Back and forth (4-6) / Build a scene (1-3) Change (1-3) / Change the mood (3-6) / Character, place, and me (4-6) / Choral reading (1-6) / Commercials

1-6) / Create a character (1-6) / Different purpose (4) / For real (1-3) / Guided imagery (K-1) / Helping circle (1-3) / How do you speak? (1-2) / How was your day? (4-6) / Human computer (3) / In the mood (1-3) Live art (1-6) / Making toast (4-5) / Mannequin challenge (1-6) / Minor to major (4-6) / Opposites (1-2) Re purpose it (3-4) / Read, predict, change (1-3) / Step in–step out (4-6) / Story boards (4-6) / Using drama skills for a purpose (1-6) / We need someone else (2-3) / What happens next? (1-6) / What should you do? (1-3) / What would happen? (4-6) / What would it be like? (1-3) / What you imagine and what you know (4-6) What's the sense? (1-3) / What's your problem? (1-3) / Where are we? (1-3) / Who owns this? (1) Whose seat is it? (1-3)

Developing Facial Expression

Audition improvisation (Grade 1-6) / How can you show? (1-3) / Mannequin challenge (1-6) / Mime (1-6) P.I. for a day (4-6) / Pick a character (4-6) / Puppetry (1-6) / Staged reading (4-6) / Tableaux (1-6) / What would we look like? (1-3) / Words, face, body (1-3)

Developing Vocal Expression

Audition improvisation (Grade 1-6) / Change the meaning–word emphasis (1-6) / Change the mood 2 (1-3) Choral reading (1-6) / Dynamics (1) / Escalate (2-6) / How can you show? (1-3) / How do you speak? (1-2) / Puppetry (1-6) / Radio plays (4-6) / Reader's theatre (4-6) / Staged reading (4-6) / Storytelling (3 to 6) What did you say? (4-6) / Who is this for? (4-6) / Words, face, body (1-3)

Drama Forms

Choral reading (Grade 1-6) / Cultural celebrations (1-6) / Greek theatre (5) / Interviews/talk shows (4-6) Masks (4-6) / Mime (1-6) / Puppetry (1-6) / Radio plays (4-6) / Recap (1-3) / Soundscape (1-6) / Storytelling (3-6) Survey says (1-6) / Tableaux (1-6) / What's the difference? (4-6)

Elements of Drama

Back and forth (4-6) / Change (1-3) / Change the meaning–word emphasis (1-6) / Change the mood (3-6) / Character on the wall (1-6) / Character, place and me (4-6) / Character sketch (4-6) / Character tree (6) Create a character (1-6) / Dynamics (1) / Five things to know about me (1-6) / How can you tell? (4-6) In the mood (4-6) / Laryngitis (1-3) / Orchestra (4-6) / Press release for a play (4-6) / Set (4-5) / Take a minute (4-6) / Two sides of the coin (4-6) /

Focus/ Stay in Role

Art Gallery (Grade 4-6) / Audition improvisation (1-6) / Live art (1-6) / Make me laugh (1-3) / Staged reading (4-6) / Wax museum (1-6)

Good Audience/ Listener

Audience chameleon (Grade 1-2) / Good audience/ listener (K-3)

Improvisation

Hot and cold (Grade 1-3) / Re purpose it (3-4) / Shopping spree (1-3)

Interpretation

Change the meaning- word emphasis (Grade 1-6) / Change the mood 2 (1-3) / How can you tell? (4-6) Step in–step out (4-6)

Mistakes while Performing

Fake it till you make it (Grade 4-6)

Peer Critiquing

Film performances (4-6) / Smile/frown (1-3) / Two stars and a wish (1-3)

Performing

Warm up exercises (Grade 1-6)

Personal Connections to Their Lives and Community Past and Present

A day in the life of (Grade 1-3) / Audience chameleon (1-2) / Back and forth (4-6) / Build a scene (1-3) Create a character (1-6) / Cultural presentations (1-6) / Hot and cold (1-3) / How do you speak? (1-2) Move it (1-3) / Real or not real (1) / Role play imagination (1-6) / Show me (1-2) / This is not a drill (1-6)

INDEX

Wax museum (1-6) / What should I wear? / What's the sense (1-3)

Point of View
Advice hallway (1-6) / Change the meaning- word emphasis (1-6)
Conflict resolution fairy (1-3) / Consequences (1-6) / Fairy tale therapy (2-4)
Minor to major (4-6) / Pick a character (4-6) / Put yourself in his shoes, hat or shirt (4-6)
Two sides of the coin (4-6) / Switch (1-3) / What's your issue? (5-6)
Who is your audience? (4-6) / Why did you do that? (4-6) / Voices in the head (4-6)

Predictions
Read, predict, change (1-3)

Presentations
Survey says (1-6)

Presenting
Change the mood (3-6)

Problem-solving
Advice hallway (1-6) / Step in- step out (4-6) / What should you do? (1-3)

Reality Versus Fiction
Human computer (grade 3) / Real or not real (1)

Retelling Stories
And then this happened… (1-3) / Change (1-3) / Choral reading (1-6) / Minor to major (4-6)
Puppetry (1-6) / Radio plays (4-6) / Reader's theatre (4-6) / Recap (1-3) / Same thing four ways (3-6)
Storytelling (3-6) / Two sides of the coin (4-6) / Tableaux (1-6)

Role Play
Build a scene (1- 3) / Conflict resolution fairy tale (1-3) / In and out (4-6)
Role playing (1-6)

Sequencing of Events
A day in the life of (1-3) / Making toast (4-5) / Recap (1-3)

Symbols
Symbolism (6)

Technology
Public speaking (4-6) / Radio plays (4-6)

Written Assignments
Press release for a play (4-6)

PEER CHANGER

by Jackie Bennett

SCENE 1

ETHAN is sitting at a table in his kitchen doing his homework. OMARI walks in.

OMARI
Hey Ethan. Do you want to come play at my house?

ETHAN
I have to finish my homework first.

OMARI
How long is that going to take?

ETHAN
Not long if you help me.

OMARI
I'm not doing your homework.

ETHAN
I don't want you to do it for me. I have to write a four sentence paragraph about what I want to be when I grow up and I need two people to peer edit for me.

OMARI
What's that?

ETHAN
Didn't you do this with your teacher?

OMARI
No. Is it a game?

ETHAN
Peer edit means you get a friend, that would be you Omari, to read what you wrote and fix any mistakes or make suggestions to make it better.

OMARI
Oh yah. We did that.

ETHAN
So, will you do it?

OMARI
Do what?

ETHAN
Peer edit my paragraph so I can go to your house.

OMARI
Sure. Give it to me.

ETHAN
Here's a green pen to mark it with.

ETHAN hands him the paper and pen, OMARI makes marks on the page while he reads it out loud. Words in italics are to be read from the paper.

OMARI
When I grow up I wants be a vet. Shouldn't it be 'want to be a vet'? And there's no capital at the beginning of your sentence. *I want to be a vet because I like animals.* Is that how you spell because 'cause I don't know. *I would like to work with animals that people have been mean to.* You forgot a period. *If I was a vet then I could help animals that no one else wants.* Since when do you want to be a vet anyway? I thought you were going to own a hamburger place.

ETHAN
That was last month.

OMARI
I don't know. I think it would be too sad being a vet cause you'd have to tell people their pets died. Why don't you write about the hamburger place?

ETHAN
Because I don't want to do that anymore. So is it OK now or is there something else I should change?

OMARI
Looks good to me.

ETHAN
Thanks. Just let me write a note and then I can leave it for my brother to be my second peer editor. [*He writes as he says out loud...*] I need a peer editor for my homework? Can you do it for me? Use the green pen. Thanks, Ethan.

ETHAN puts his paper into his writing folder and sticks the note onto the outside.

ETHAN
Oh, and I better leave another note saying I'm at your place.

ETHAN writes another note and puts it on the table beside his homework. The two boys exit.

SCENE 2

Ethan's older brother JACOB enters the kitchen with his friend YUNA.

JACOB
Do you want something to eat, Yuna?

YUNA
We just ate four slices of pizza at Mazie's. Well, I ate one. You ate three. You can't still be hungry, Jacob.

Playscripts

JACOB
So, is that a no?

YUNA
No thanks.

JACOB gets a box of crackers and starts eating them.

YUNA
There's a note here from your brother. He says he needs a peer editor for his homework.

JACOB
I hate it when he asks me to do that.

YUNA
Why? He's your little brother. Why won't you help him with his homework?

JACOB
I don't mind helping him with his homework. I just don't like it when he asks me to check something. If I make any suggestions, he gets all defensive and says I'm always criticizing him.

YUNA
Well he's not here so just make the changes and leave it for him. Then he can't say anything.

JACOB
I suppose. Give me the folder.

YUNA passes the folder to JACOB. They sit at the table. JACOB reads the assignment, again reading the words in italics out loud.

JACOB
When I grow up I want to be a vet. He should put 'veterinarian' otherwise it sounds like he wants to be in the army.

YUNA
It would also be better if he said, "When I grow up the job I would

like to have is to be a veterinarian." It makes it clearer what he is talking about.

JACOB
Sounds good.

He makes the changes and then continues.

JACOB
I want to be a vet because I like animals. That's a bit general. Who doesn't like animals? Ummm, what do you think?

YUNA
Yah. How about something like, "I want to be a vet because I have always enjoyed spending time with animals. My family has three dogs and I am good at looking after them."

JACOB
Hey, you're good at this.

He writes down what she says.

JACOB
OK. Do the next sentence. *I would like to work with animals that people have been mean to.*

YUNA
That's easy. "Particularly I would like to work with animals that cruel people have abused." What's next?

JACOB
The last sentence is, *If I was a vet then I could help animals that no one else wants.*

YUNA
That's it? He needs a concluding sentence. Leave what he wrote but add, "That's why when I grow up I would like to be a veterinarian."

JACOB scribbles the last sentence.

JACOB
Great. Let's go to the library so we can do our own homework.

YUNA
Sure, but this looks a mess now. He won't be able to read your writing. I'll just rewrite it for him with the changes.

JACOB
OK and I'll write a note to let Mom know we're at the library and have eaten already.

YUNA quickly rewrites the story and puts it back in the folder. Jacob puts a note beside Ethan's. They leave.

SCENE 3

DAD enters the room.

DAD
Susan? Are you home? Jacob? Ethan? Anyone?

DAD looks at his watch.

DAD
I wonder where everyone is?

DAD sees the pile of notes. He reads each one as he picks it up.

DAD
'Gone to Omari's, Ethan.' 'At library, had dinner, Jacob.' 'I've gone to the dry cleaner's, Susan.' 'I need a peer editor for my homework? Can you do it for me? Use the green pen. Thanks, Ethan.' I'll leave that for Susan. She's much better at that sort of thing.

DAD sits at the table and plays imaginary drums with his fingers. He looks at the folder and gives a sigh.

DAD
Oh, why not.

He takes the paper out of the folder and reads it. He immediately picks up the green pen and starts to make corrections. His wife comes in carrying a bag of groceries just as he's finishing writing a good copy.

MOM
Hi Mike. You're home early. What have you got there? Doing your homework?

DAD
It's Ethan's.

MOM
Mike. We have talked about this before. He's not going to learn anything if you keep doing his work for him.

DAD
I'm not, Susan. He left a note saying he needed a peer editor, so I thought I'd give it a try. Here, read this and tell me what you think.

He hands the paper to his wife.

MOM
It's in your writing.

DAD
Actually, it's printing since he can't read cursive very well and I only rewrote it so he could read all my corrections.

MOM picks up the paper and reads it out loud.

MOM

When I have matured into a young man the job I would most be suited for would be a veterinarian. I would excel at being a veterinarian because I have always enjoyed spending time with animals. My family has three dogs and I have assisted in providing excellent and loving care for them. It is of particular importance to me to rescue animals that have been abused by cruel people. There are increasingly large numbers of animals being abandoned by their selfish owners and I would like to offer those animals a hopeful future. That's why when I grow up I would like to be a veterinarian.

(puts paper down) This doesn't sound anything like something Ethan would write. Does he even want to be a vet?

DAD

I hardly changed anything. I just spruced up the wording a bit to make it more professional.

MOM

Let me see the original.

He hands her the copy YUNA wrote. She reads it.

MOM

When I grow up the job I would like to do is be a veterinarian. I want to be a veterinarian because I have always enjoyed spending time with animals. My family has three dogs and I am good at looking after them. Particularly I would like to work with animals that have been abused by cruel people. If I was a vet then I could help animals that no one else wants. That's why when I grow up I would like to be a veterinarian. Well, I'm impressed. His writing has really improved.

DAD

See, I didn't change much at all. I just enhanced it.

MOM

Well, Ethan can decide which changes he'd like to use. Since you're so good at helping with homework, how would you like to help me with dinner?

DAD
I'd be happy to.

SCENE 4

ETHAN enters the kitchen where his parents are playing cards.

ETHAN
Hi Mom. Hi Dad. Thanks for letting me stay for dinner with Omari's family even though it's a school night.

MOM
You did such a great job on your assignment that I thought you deserved a treat.

ETHAN
Really?

DAD
Yes, your mother and I were very impressed by the improvement you have shown in your writing. Only a few small suggestions were needed.

ETHAN
Cool. Thanks.

MOM
You can read them in the morning. It's late. You better get on up to bed.

ETHAN
OK, night Mom, night Dad.

MOM and DAD
Good night son.

SCENE 5

ETHAN and OMARI are standing outside their school, raincoats and backpacks on, waiting for the bell to ring.

OMARI
Do you want to play soccer until the bell rings?

ETHAN
It's too wet.

OMARI
Yah. It rained buckets last night.

ETHAN
I was hoping it would be a rain day and school would be cancelled.

OMARI
We don't get rain days.

ETHAN
I know. But since it wasn't going to snow, I thought maybe we could have a rain day instead.

OMARI
We're not that lucky. Did Jacob peer edit your paragraph?

ETHAN
Yes, and my parents said it was really good.

OMARI
Do you want me to check it one more time?

ETHAN
Sure.

ETHAN takes his folder out of his backpack and hands it to OMARI. OMARI opens it and starts to read the top page.

OMARI
When I have mat, mat, mattered? into a yo, yo, yo ung man the job I would most be suited for would be a vet, vet ner nian. This makes no sense.

ETHAN
What are you reading? That's not what I wrote.

OMARI hands the folder to him. ETHAN looks at the top paper in confusion.

ETHAN
I didn't write this. I can't even read half the words. And it's my Dad's writing. I didn't ask him to peer edit for me. When he said it only needed a couple of changes I thought he was talking about what Jacob did. This is like twice as much as I wrote.

ETHAN takes the folder and looks through it.

ETHAN
Where did all this paper come from? (*He starts to read the next paper.*) *When I grow up the job I would like to do is be a veterinarian. I want to be a veterinarian because I have always enjoyed spending time with animals.* I didn't write this one either. I don't even know whose writing it is. (*He looks at the next paper.*) This is Jacob's writing and this other one is the one you corrected. What am I going to do? If I read Dad's changes, everyone will laugh at me.

OMARI
That's if you can even read it.

ETHAN
I am doomed!

ETHAN waves the folder around in frustration and watches in horror as the papers go flying up in the air.

ETHAN
Ahhh. Quick, catch them. Oh no, they're falling in the puddle.

He falls to his knees as he grabs at his papers.

> OMARI
> They're all wet. Will they be OK?

> ETHAN
> The green ink is running all over the place. Even if it dries it won't be any good. What am I going to do?

> OMARI
> You can say the dog ate it. Or, in this case, the puddle ate it. Or you could just rewrite it quickly.

> ETHAN
> I guess I'll have to.

> OMARI
> Hurry up before the bell rings.

ETHAN uses OMARI'S back as a surface to write on.

> ETHAN
> I'm done. I think I remembered all the capitals and stuff. What do you think?

ETHAN hands the paper to OMARI.

> OMARI
> Looks good to me.

SCENE 6

Students are sitting at desks. The other characters not in the scene can be dressed as students or you can just pretend there are other students at their desks.

> MRS. HARRIS
> Ethan. Will you share with us what you want to be when you grow up?

ETHAN stands up, clears his throat and reads his paper.

ETHAN

When I grow up I want to be a vet. I want to be a vet because I like animals. I want to work with animals that people have been mean to. If I was a vet then I could help animals that no one else wants.

MRS. HARRIS

Well done, Ethan. I am so proud of you. Your writing has really improved.

THE END

PRODUCTION NOTES FOR *PEER CHANGER*

CHARACTERS
Ethan, Omari, Jacob, Yuna, Dad, Mom, Mrs. Harris

SETTING
Ethan's kitchen, school yard, classroom

PROPS
green pen
paper
a good copy of the homework and a ruined copy
sticky notes
writing folder
box of crackers
deck of cards

COSTUMES
Regular clothes, backpacks

SET
Table (can be used as kitchen table and school desk), 2 chairs

THE BASEBALL CAP

By Jackie Bennett

PETER, JAKE, CHARLOTTE, QUINTON, STANLEY and MADDIE are standing in the living room.

PETER
It's my birthday and I want to play sardines.

JAKE
Who said you couldn't?

PETER
I saw you roll your eyes when I suggested it.

JAKE
Are you making fun of my eyes?

CHARLOTTE
I personally think they're gross.

JAKE
You think my eyes are gross?

CHARLOTTE
Not your eyes, Jake! Sardines. They're so slimy and smelly.

QUINTON
My mom makes me eat them. The thought of them makes me gag!

MADDIE
Really? I love them. On toast, with mayo. I could eat them every day.

PETER
You guys are crazy. I never…

JAKE
So now you think I'm crazy too.

PETER
I didn't say you're crazy.

JAKE
You just did.

STANLEY
Yah. You did.

MADDIE
Although technically he said we're all crazy.

PETER
Oh my goodness. You *are* crazy. All I wanted to do was…

JAKE
See? I was right. He thinks we're crazy.

JAKE grabs the hat off PETER'S head. PETER tries to get it back. JAKE throws it to STANLEY.

PETER
Give me my hat back, Stanley.

PETER tries to get his hat, but STANLEY throws it to JAKE.

PETER
I mean it. Give me my hat back.

JAKE
It's just a stinky hat. Maybe I should throw it in the garbage where it belongs.

PETER
NO! You can't do that. Give it back.

JAKE
Not until you say we're not crazy.

PETER
It's just an expression.

JAKE throws the hat to QUINTON.

PETER
You're not crazy. Give me my hat back.

JAKE
Say pretty please.

MADDIE grabs the hat and hands it to PETER who jams it back on his head. There's a moment of silence when no one knows what to say.

CHARLOTTE
Well, whatever. I don't care if it is your birthday, Peter. I'm not eating sardines.

PETER
I never said you have to eat them. It's a game.

MADDIE
Oh, that's disappointing. I would have enjoyed that. Much more interesting than the usual pizza.

STANLEY
But I like pizza. You said we were going to have pizza. Why aren't we going to have pizza? I won't eat sardines.

PETER
For the last time, we're not eating the sardines. It's a game called sardines.

QUINTON
I don't think I even want to play with them.

JAKE
I have a soccer game later. I don't want to go there smelling like fish guts.

PETER
We're not playing with them. It's just called that.

STANLEY
Is there pizza or not?

QUINTON
Never heard of the game.

MADDIE
Me neither.

CHARLOTTE
Oh wait, is that the game that's like hide and seek but backwards?

PETER
Yes. We all start…

STANLEY
Won't it be kind of hard to hide if we're walking backwards?

PETER
One, two, three …

JAKE
Wait, you're going too fast. Give us a chance to hide.

All the kids run around in confusion.

PETER
GET BACK HERE!

They come back.

MADDIE
What's wrong?

QUINTON
I had the perfect spot.

PETER
I didn't say, "Go hide."

QUINTON
But you started to count.

PETER
I was counting to five because I am getting so mad.

MADDIE
Why were you getting mad?

STANLEY
'Cause we have to eat sardines instead of pizza.

PETER
I am mad because no one is listening to what I am …

JAKE
We're listening.

PETER
… trying to say.

CHARLOTTE
What ARE you trying to say? I am so confused.

STANLEY
Me too. Is there pizza or not?

PETER
I am saying that we are going to play a game called sardines. And when we are finished, we will not be eating sardines. We will eat pizza and cake. Charlotte will tell you how to play and I am going to hide somewhere far away from you guys.

PETER leaves the room.

JAKE
What's with him?

The Baseball Cap

QUINTON
You insulted his sardines.

STANLEY
But we're eating pizza, aren't we?

JAKE
Not anymore if he's mad at us.

STANLEY
You're the one who touched his grungy hat.

CHARLOTTE
He's not mad. Just frustrated.

JAKE
Well, he went off in a snit, didn't he?

CHARLOTTE
He went to hide.

MADDIE
If he's not mad, why's he hiding?

CHARLOTTE
He's supposed to hide. That's how you play the game. One person hides, that would be Peter, and I'd say with the amount of time we're wasting he has found a really good place. Then we count to one hundred and then we all go look for him.

STANLEY
I'm not looking for him if we're not having pizza anymore.

JAKE
Stanley! Will you stop with the pizza? He said we're having pizza. So, we're having pizza.

STANLEY
OK. Let's go look for him. He might eat it all if we don't find him quick.

They all start to leave together except Charlotte.

CHARLOTTE
You can't go yet. I haven't told you all the rules yet. We go look for him by ourselves. If we find him, we join him in his hiding spot, and we all cram together like sardines in a can until the last person finds us.

MADDIE
That sounds fun.

STANLEY
Do we walk backwards when we're looking for him?

CHARLOTTE
NO!

JAKE
Then this sounds stupid, Charlotte. Aren't we a bit old to be playing games?

MADDIE
I'm not. And it's Peter's party.

CHARLOTTE
Let's go find him.

They all leave the room. Peter enters and hides under a table.

PETER
I hope they never find me. This is the worst party ever. I don't even know any of them but Mom said I had to invite them so I can meet new kids. Why'd we have to move across the country two weeks before my birthday? And I told Mom no one would want to play sardines.

CHARLOTTE and JAKE enter. They don't notice Peter hiding.

CHARLOTTE
Stop following me.

JAKE
I'm not. I'm just looking in the same places as you.

CHARLOTTE
Well stop. It's more fun if we find him at different times.

JAKE
This is boring. I'd rather be at Hakum's house. He has lots of computer games.

CHARLOTTE
Then why'd you come if it's so much better over there?

JAKE
Mom said I had to since he's new and doesn't know anyone yet. Why'd the rest of you come? You don't know him either.

CHARLOTTE
I guess he invited us because we're in his class. I mean, who else is he going to invite if he doesn't know anyone. He's seems OK.

JAKE
He's kind of strange. I mean, who likes eating sardines? And what's with that hat? Did you see how he almost cried when I took it? What a baby. Why does he always wear it anyways? It's like he thinks he's some kind of great player. He probably can't even play.

CHARLOTTE
Maybe he really likes that team. I'm getting hungry so let's go find him.

JAKE
Sure. (*He starts to follow Charlotte.*)

CHARLOTTE
Ahem. Don't follow me.

JAKE rolls his eyes and leaves the room.
CHARLOTTE walks through the room. She walks past Peter, freezes, and slowly walks back.

CHARLOTTE
Peter. Um. Hi. I guess I found you.

She joins him in his hiding spot. They sit in silence for a few moments.

CHARLOTTE
Would it be possible you didn't hear us talking?

Peter shakes his head.

CHARLOTTE
I'm sorry. We were just like, you know, um, well, talking. We didn't mean anything by it.

Silence

PETER
The hat is my dad's. He said I could wear it until he comes home.

CHARLOTTE
Oh. Where is he?

PETER
He's overseas. He's a soldier.

CHARLOTTE
How long has been gone?

PETER
Almost seven months.

CHARLOTTE
You must miss him.

PETER
Yah.

CHARLOTTE
Is that why you wear that hat all the time?

PETER
I don't wear it all the time. I'm not allowed to wear it in school. I just like to remember my dad.

CHARLOTTE
Why? Do you forget him sometimes?

PETER
No! I just feel bad cause sometimes I forget to think of him.

CHARLOTTE
You can't think of someone every second or your brain would get too full thinking about everyone you know and then there'd be no room for anything else.

PETER
What?

CHARLOTTE
I don't think about my dad all day long. It doesn't mean I don't like him anymore.

PETER
I won't ever stop liking him. I just wear the hat 'cause it's like he's with me.

CHARLOTTE
Are you worried about him?

PETER
Sometimes. Especially when I hear on the news about other soldiers who have died. I always get scared because they never say at first who it is, just that another soldier was killed.

QUINTON enters the room.

QUINTON
I can hear you guys talking, you know.

QUINTON slides under the table to join them.

QUINTON
So, who got killed?

CHARLOTTE
Quinton, be nice.

QUINTON
I am being nice. I just wanted to know who you were talking about.

CHARLOTTE
We're talking about Peter's dad. He's a soldier and Peter is scared for him.

PETER
I didn't say I was scared. Nothing scares me.

STANLEY sneaks in while PETER is talking and bangs on top of the table. PETER, CHARLOTTE and QUINTON scream.

STANLEY
I found you.

CHARLOTTE
Well, you're supposed to be quiet about it. Maddie and Alex haven't found us yet.

STANLEY crawls under the table with them.

STANLEY
They'll find you anyways. You guys are making enough noise with all your chattering for anyone in the house to find you.

CHARLOTTE turns to PETER.

CHARLOTTE
Well, I know I'd be scared if one of my parents was in another country where there's fighting.

The Baseball Cap

STANLEY
Who's fighting?

QUINTON
Peter's dad. He's a soldier.

STANLEY
Wow. He must be really brave.

PETER
Yah. He says he doesn't feel brave; he just wants to help make our world a better place.

CHARLOTTE
That's why Peter wears that hat. It's his dad's.

STANLEY
Oh. I thought you just liked baseball. Sorry I tried to keep it from you. I didn't know.

PETER
That's OK.

CHARLOTTE
Next time you talk to your dad or email or whatever you're allowed to do, will you say hi for me and say thanks for making our world better.

QUINTON and STANLEY
Me too.

JAKE enters the room and crawls under the table.

JAKE
You cheated, Peter.

PETER
No I didn't.

JAKE
Yah. Charlotte and I looked in here and you weren't here, so you changed hiding spots.

CHARLOTTE
Umm, actually he was here. We just didn't see him.

JAKE
No, because we were talking about… Ohhhhhh.

CHARLOTTE nods her head. JAKE whispers to CHARLOTTE.

JAKE
Did he hear?

CHARLOTTE
Everything.

JAKE
Sorry I said that stuff, Peter. Your house has been empty for so long I am glad you moved in. And about the hat, you can wear whatever you want.

CHARLOTTE
The hat is his dad's. He's a soldier and has been gone for a long time.

JAKE
Oh. I guess I'd wear my dad's hat too if he was gone.

MADDIE enters the room and stands by the table.

MADDIE
Am I the last one?

The kids under the table crawl out.

JAKE
What took you so long, Maddie? We've been here for ages.

The Baseball Cap

CHARLOTTE
You have not. Jake just got here.

QUINTON
Does that mean we can eat now? I'm starving.

PETER
Have a seat and I'll be back in a moment with food.

They sit at the table they have been hiding under. PETER comes back in with a tray of food.

PETER
Food is ready. Sardines for everyone!

STANLEY
What? Is he joking? Are you joking?

CHARLOTTE looks at the food.

CHARLOTTE
No jokes. Sardines it is.

STANLEY
Seriously?

PETER
Yup! Pizza in the shape of sardines. Let's eat!

THE END

PRODUCTION NOTES FOR *THE BASEBALL CAP*

CHARACTERS
Peter, Jake, Charlotte, Quinton, Stanley and Maddie

LOCATION
First floor of a house

PROPS

- A table big enough for 5 people to sit under and chairs positioned on three sides. If the play is being done in a classroom raise the table up so the audience can see what's happening or have the audience sit on the floor.
- Pizza box
- Baseball cap

SPIDERS, DOGS AND UNDERWEAR

by Jackie Bennett

DAPHNE, MAEVE, TIC TAC and JACKIE are practicing dance steps for their music video they are making for a class project. AMICA comes running in very excited.

>AMICA
>Spider…

DAPHNE jumps on to a chair.

>DAPHNE
>Ahhh! Spider! I hate spiders.

JACKIE jumps forward with some karate moves.

>JACKIE
>Jackie Chan will scare the spiders away.

>AMICA
>No Daphne! Spider…

>DAPHNE
>Ahh! Get it away from me. Where is it? Is it on me?

JACKIE does some more karate moves.

>JACKIE
>I will save you from the scary spider.

>AMICA
>No! That word you don't like plus 'dog' is coming to our class.

TIC TAC hides behind JACKIE.

TIC TAC
Dog? Where? I thought dogs weren't allowed in school. I don't like dogs. Once when I was tobogganing a large dog ran across the hill, bit me on the leg and ran away with my pant leg.

MAEVE
I remember that. Everyone thought you were screaming because you were going down the hill too fast.

JACKIE
Was your leg bleeding all over the white snow?

TIC TAC
No.

JACKIE
Too bad. That would have looked awesome.

MAEVE
But Tic Tac needed five stitches.

TIC TAC
How'd you know I needed stitches, Maeve?

MAEVE
You brought your leg for show and tell.

TIC TAC
Oh yah.

AMICA
Who cares about stitches? Spider…

DAPHNE
Ahh! Spider!

JACKIE
Jackie to the rescue.

AMICA
Will you stop that? There isn't a spider so get down from that chair before you fall off.

DAPHNE gets down.

AMICA
And Jackie, just 'cause your name happens to be Jackie Chan doesn't mean you're a karate expert.

TIC TAC
Actually, Jackie does takes Karate. He's got a belt and everything.

JACKIE
Yes, and I play hockey, and basically anything where I get to use up all my energy. I have lots of energy.

DAPHNE
So why are you trying to scare me, Amica? You know I don't like spiders.

AMICA
I'm not trying to scare you. I am trying to tell you that someone whose name is spelled s.p.i.d.e.r and ends with a d.o.g. is coming to our class.

JACKIE
Spiderdog is coming to our class? How do you know?

AMICA
How come when Jackie says spider…

DAPHNE
Ahh! Spider!

AMICA
… dog,

TIC TAC
Dog?
AMICA

… you don't scream in terror?

DAPHNE
He says it less scary than you.

MAEVE
Why would Spiderdog be coming here? Isn't he like the most famous performer on YouTube?

TIC TAC
YouTube? That's just how he started. He's world famous now, in and out of the tube. Is he really coming here?

AMICA
Apparently he heard we were making a music video for class with his song *You Don't Scare Me*.

MAEVE
Is he mad we're using it?

JACKIE
I hope not. I like it. *(He starts to rap.)*
When something scares me
I won't let it drop me
Won't let it stop me

AMICA
His blog says he wants to do the video with us.

MAEVE
Why?

JACKIE does some karate moves.

JACKIE
Maybe he heard of my famous karate moves.

TIC TAC
Famous to who?

AMICA

All I know is what I read on his blog. He's coming here sometime before his concert to help us with our video.

DAPHNE
Oh my goodness! He is just the cutest guy ever. I can't believe we're going to meet him.

JACKIE
Oh, he's so cute. Kissy, kissy, kiss, kiss.

He kisses the air and turns around and bumps into SPIDERDOG who has entered without them noticing.

SPIDERDOG
Hi. I'm Spider…

DAPHNE
Ahh! Spider!

DAPHNE faints. SPIDERDOG looks at her in concern. AMICA steps over her and holds out her hand.

AMICA
Hi. I'm Amica. I'm your biggest fan.

SPIDERDOG
Shouldn't we help your friend?

AMICA
Oh, Jackie can help her.

JACKIE does a few karate moves and helps DAPHNE up.

JACKIE
You must be used to girls screaming when they see you.

SPIDERDOG
You OK?

DAPHNE nods her head. AMICA whispers to SPIDERDOG.

AMICA
She's scared of spiders.

TIC TAC
Really scared. Just the word sends her screaming. Check it out. Daphne! There's a huge spider on your head.

DAPHNE
Ahhh! Get it off me! Get it off me!

TIC TAC
Relax, Daphne. I'm just joking.

MAEVE
I don't think she's laughing, Tic Tac.

JACKIE
I think she's going to barf.

DAPHNE
I'm OK. Just keep the spiders away.

AMICA
How are we supposed to work with HIM if you're going to freak out every time someone starts to say his name?

MAEVE
I think she should leave if she can't handle it. This is a once in a lifetime opportunity and I don't want it ruined by her phobia.

JACKIE
That's not nice.

MAEVE
Well, what else are we supposed to do?

SPIDERDOG
Do I get any say in this?
AMICA

Oh. Sure.

SPIDERDOG
Daphne, right? You know I'm not really a bug with eight legs.

DAPHNE nods her head.

JACKIE
He's not really a dog either, Tic Tac.

TIC TAC
Who said he was?

JACKIE
I remember you were scared when you thought a dog was coming.

SPIDERDOG
You're scared of dogs?

TIC TAC
Only if they want to bite me, or rip my pants off.

SPIDERDOG
Have I ever got the wrong name for this group.

MAEVE
There's nothing you can do about it. If that's your name, then that's your name and anyone who can't handle it should go, and those of us who can will stay behind and do the video with you.

DAPHNE
I can't help it if I'm scared of spiders.

SPIDERDOG
Everyone is scared of something.

MAEVE
I'm not.

AMICA
What about underwear?

JACKIE
Really, Maeve? You're scared of underwear?

MAEVE
Thanks a lot, Amica. That was supposed to be a secret.

TIC TAC
How can someone be scared of underwear?

AMICA
She thought the pictures of Tinkerbell on her underwear were real and she screamed every time she saw them.

JACKIE
You're scared of Tinkerbell?

MAEVE
That was when I was like two. I so got over that years ago.

SPIDERDOG
The point is, everyone is scared of something.

DAPHNE
What are you scared of?

SPIDERDOG
I used to be freaked out by spaghetti.

TIC TAC
How can someone be scared of spaghetti?

JACKIE
How can someone be scared of underwear?

MAEVE
Not anymore.

SPIDERDOG
When I was small someone told me that the noodles were bloodsucking worms and all the sauce was blood from their last victim.

MAEVE
You know that's not true, don't you?

SPIDERDOG
Of course, but I still don't like spaghetti, but I'll eat it if I have to. Being scared of something is not a big deal unless it stops you from doing things you should be doing.

AMICA
Like doing this video. Well Daphne, as Maeve said, there's nothing we can do about his name so you maybe should just go home.

SPIDERDOG
There is actually.

MAEVE
Really?

SPIDERDOG
The bug with eight legs and animal with four legs is not my real name.

DAPHNE
It's not?

AMICA
What is it? I can't wait to tell everyone I was the first person to know your real name.

SPIDERDOG
You wouldn't be the first person. My parents know.

TIC TAC
You have parents?

SPIDERDOG
Yes, and two brothers who also know my real name.

TIC TAC
So, you weren't born in a bat cave?

SPIDERDOG
What have you been reading? I'm not some cartoon person. I just don't want people to know my real name.

DAPHNE
Why not?

JACKIE
Are you scared of your name?

SPIDERDOG
No. I like my name, but I prefer to keep my personal life private from my performing life. But I will make a deal with you. If you promise not to tell anyone my real name, then you can call me that. And then that way, I can do the video with all of you. Agreed?

DAPHNE, TIC TAC, MAEVE and JACKIE
Sure

They all turn to look at AMICA.

AMICA
OK. I won't say anything. I promise. But I don't see how changing your name is supposed to stop her being scared of crawly things.

SPIDERDOG
It doesn't. It just helps her find a way to do something even when she is scared. You're not too scared to do the video with me, are you?

DAPHNE
I wasn't scared of you, it's just the thought of spiders.

SPIDERDOG
So, you're cool now?

DAPHNE
Yes.

MAEVE
Does that mean you're not going to tell us your real name anymore?

AMICA
Yah. Come on. Tell us please.

SPIDERDOG
It's Todd.

JACKIE
Really? Cool. I guess that's not going to make anyone scream and jump on a chair.

TIC TAC
Except for the girls who are in love with you.

AMICA
So, Todd? Are you going to tell us why a big star like you is coming to our school to help us on a class video?

MAEVE
Not that we're not super excited you're here.

AMICA
I mean, why? This just doesn't happen in normal life.

SPIDERDOG
Ms. Beecham is a friend of mine.

TIC TAC
You know our teacher? How did that happen? How come she never told us?

SPIDERDOG
More secrets than I might tell you someday. Meanwhile, let's get to work. Ms. Beecham said you already have some great dance moves. Do you want to show them to me?

JACKIE
Will you do the words? After all, it's your song.

They get into format, the five students dance while SPIDERDOG raps.

SPIDERDOG
When something scares me
I won't let it drop me
Won't let it stop me
Thunder and lightning
I won't let it drop me
Won't let it stop me
Darkness and noises
I won't let it drop me
Won't let it stop me

THE END

PRODUCTION NOTES FOR *SPIDERS. DOGS AND UNDERWEAR*

CHARACTERS
Daphne, Amica, Maeve, Jackie, Spiderdog, Tic Tac

PROPS
A chair

SETTING
Classroom

COSTUMES
Regular clothes for the students
and something rapper-like for Spiderdog

THE TIME MACHINE

By Jackie Bennett

Setting: Garage at Amber's home. Current time.

AMBER is working on a large time machine and PIKE, SAM, GERRIT and CHELSEA are sitting on chairs off to the side, reading, playing with games, or listening to music.

AMBER
Guys! Come quick. It works.

SAM
Are you serious?

AMBER
I think so. Everything checks out OK. Just have to test it.

GERRIT
You said that the last fourteen times.

AMBER
Yes, but this time I am certain it will work.

CHELSEA
You said that the last fourteen times too.

AMBER
It will work. Who's coming?

SAM
Where are we going?

AMBER
Anywhere you want.

PIKE
How about ancient Greece? We could go to the first Olympics.

AMBER
We can't do that. Girls weren't allowed at the Olympics then.

CHELSEA
Why?

AMBER
Because the athletes didn't wear clothes.

PIKE
Seriously? Yo dude. I don't need to see that.

GERRIT
What about medieval times? We could be knights and have sword fights.

CHELSEA
Why does it have to be somewhere violent?

PIKE
The guys can have sword fights and the girls can do embroidery or whatever girls did back then.

CHELSEA
I'm sure we had more important things to do than just embroidery.

AMBER
Ya, like stitching you up after you almost kill each other.

CHELSEA
I think we should go somewhere that isn't much different than now. I don't want to die on our first trip.

AMBER
I'm not planning on dying on any trip. But Chelsea is right. We should pick somewhere safe for our first time.

PIKE
You guys are so boring. Fine. What about the sixties, man?

AMBER
We can see the sixties on television. How about going back to pioneer times?

PIKE
Yah. I guess. Just not to school. Remember when we went to the pioneer village with our class? I had to stand with my arms stretched out for an hour.

GERRIT
That's because you were talking when you weren't supposed to.

PIKE
I thought my arms were going to fall off.

GERRIT
They did tell us we had to follow the rules of pioneer times.

CHELSEA
At least you didn't have to stand on your tiptoes with your braids pinned to the wall.

GERRIT
That's your own fault because you were texting during class.

CHELSEA
Since they didn't have cell phones during pioneer times I thought I wouldn't be breaking any rules.

AMBER
You don't have to worry about it because today is Saturday so there won't be school.

PIKE
Are you sure?

AMBER
No, but if we did end up in school at least we'd meet kids our own age. And we know all the rules even if some people don't follow them.

PIKE
I guess. Sure. Why not?

AMBER
Ok. Then step right on into the world's first time machine and prepare to make history.

They crowd into the dark time machine. They either close a door or pull a curtain across so the audience doesn't see them.

GERRIT
Why didn't you build lights inside this thing?

AMBER
I didn't want to waste power.

The machine shakes and makes noises until finally it stops. Turn off the lights so the stage is dark. ELIZABETH sneaks into the back of the machine without being seen by the audience.

AMBER
We're there! Everyone OK?

Everyone says sure, great, etc.

CHELSEA
I can't believe we made it.

SAM
Let's go!

AMBER
Hang on till I get our emergency kit. We don't know what will be out there. (She picks up a box.) OK, open the door and prepare to be a pioneer.

They open the time machine door and come out.

GERRIT
It's dark. Did we travel back to nighttime?

AMBER
No. I set the dial to a.m.

PIKE
Then why can't we see anything?

AMBER
Maybe I blew a fuse.

SAM
They had fuses back then?

AMBER
No. The machine does, and it didn't work.

SAM
Ahhh. What's wrong with it this time?

AMBER
I don't know. I was sure I had everything working. Good thing I have an emergency kit.

CHELSEA
Why? Do we have an emergency?

AMBER
I need a flashlight so I can figure out how to get the power back on.

AMBER rummages through the box and brings out a flashlight, turns it on but drops it. Someone picks it up and shines it in Amber's face.

AMBER
Gerrit! Get it out of my eyes.

GERRIT
It's not me. Must be Pike.

PIKE
Why do I get blamed for everything? It's gotta be Chelsea or Sam.

CHELSEA and SAM
It's not me.

The lights come back on. They all turn slowly around and scream when they see a girl they don't know standing behind them in the time machine.

SAM
Who are you?

AMBER
And who said you could come in my garage?

GERRIT snatches the flashlight from her.

GERRIT
Give me that before you hit someone with it.

ELIZABETH
Where am I?

SAM
Yah, like we're going to believe that. You get caught breaking into Amber's house and now you act all innocent. Where am I? Huh!

ELIZABETH
I didn't break anything.

PIKE
You better not. Should we call the cops?

ELIZABETH
What are cops? Will they take me home? I want to go home.

CHELSEA
And where would that be exactly? Some place where they deal with pretend memory loss?

AMBER is jumping up and down in excitement.

AMBER
Tell me what year it is.

ELIZABETH
1868.

AMBER
YES! I knew it. The machine does work, it's just backwards.

PIKE
What are you talking about? We didn't go anywhere.

AMBER
We didn't, but SHE did.

CHELSEA
You mean she's from the past?

AMBER
You got it.

They all stare at her with interest.

CHELSEA, PIKE, GERARD and SAM
Wow!

ELIZABETH
What's happening? Who are you?

PIKE
Hey. You're not going to cry, are you? Why did you have to bring back a girl? At least a boy wouldn't bawl his eyes out.

GERRIT
You cried when your hockey team lost the tournament so don't bug her.

SAM
You cried?

PIKE
That was last year. I was younger then.

AMBER
So? You cried and no one cared. She just travelled over a hundred years and doesn't know what happened to her. I'd probably cry if I were her.

ELIZABETH
I am not crying. But I do want to know how I got here.

GERRIT
You somehow accidentally came forward in our time machine.

ELIZABETH
I don't understand.

CHELSEA
This is the year 2024.

ELIZABETH
No, it's not. It's 1868.

PIKE
You mean you're really from 1868? This is so cool. What's it like. Do you have McDonald's?

ELIZABETH
It's not that cold and there are some McDonalds living down the road from us. Do you know them?

AMBER
Sorry to tell you, but you are now in 2024. We have been trying to make this time machine work. I thought it did and we are the ones who were supposed to travel back to your time. Instead, for some reason, you came to our time instead.

ELIZABETH
I guess you think I'm not very smart if you think I'm going to believe you can change years whenever you want.

CHELSEA
Actually, it's true. Or it will be when we get the details worked out. I'm Chelsea, that's Pike, Amber, Sam and Gerrit. What's your name?

ELIZABETH
I'm leaving.

SAM
Leaving? Is that a pioneer name?

Elizabeth starts to leave.

AMBER
No. You can't leave. You can't stay here.

ELIZABETH
That doesn't make any sense.

AMBER
I meant you can't stay in 2024.

ELIZABETH
I'm going home.

GERRIT
She doesn't believe us.

PIKE
Well, then we'll prove it to you. What's your name?

ELIZABETH
Elizabeth.

SAM
That's a nicer name than Leaving.

GERRIT
Come with us, Elizabeth. You are going to be blown away.

ELIZABETH
Why, is it very windy?

AMBER
Just come with us.

At the front of the stage facing the audience AMBER and GERRIT mime pushing the garage door up so ELIZABETH can see outside. ELIZABETH stands at the opening in shock staring at a world completely different from hers.

ELIZABETH
Where did all these houses come from? I must have really wandered far from home.

AMBER
It's called a subdivision. We have lots of them.

ELIZABETH
That carriage is moving without horses.

GERRIT
That's a car. We don't use horses anymore.

ELIZABETH
There are no more horses?

SAM
Yes, just not for driving.

ELIZABETH screams as a plane flies overhead.

ELIZABETH
What is that? I've never seen such an enormous bird before.

PIKE
That's just a plane. People fly in them.

ELIZABETH
But people can't fly where I live.

AMBER
That's what we've been trying to tell you. This isn't where you live. Or maybe it used to be, I don't know. But you're here in 2024.

ELIZABETH
I don't believe it, yet everything is so different it has to be true. Unless I'm dreaming.

PIKE pinches her arm.

ELIZABETH
Ow. Why did you do that?

PIKE
That's what they do in the movies to prove someone's awake.

ELIZABETH
What's a movie?

SAM
You don't know what a movie is? When did they invent movies?

CHELSEA
Not pioneer times.

GERRIT
The point they are trying to make is if you can feel the pinch, you're not sleeping and therefore it isn't a dream.

AMBER
You came here in our machine we built.

ELIZABETH
You built it?

AMBER
Yep. It's a school project.

ELIZABETH
You make machines in class? We just learn things like reading, writing, and math.

PIKE
Most of us don't usually build machines in school. We're just in a special science class cause we're really smart.

CHELSEA'S cell phone rings causing ELIZABETH to jump.

CHELSEA
Hi Mom. *(pause to listen)* I'm at Amber's. *(pause)* We're working on our project. Can I stay? We're right in the middle of something exciting.

ELIZABETH
What is that?

CHELSEA
Mom. Say hi to my friend Elizabeth.

CHELSEA puts her phone by ELIZABETH'S ear for a moment and then takes the phone back and listens.

ELIZABETH
There is a person inside the box?

PIKE
It's a phone. That's how we talk to people who aren't here.

GERRIT
I think the phone gets invented about twenty years from your time and then you can get one.

CHELSEA
Thanks Mom. See you later.

ELIZABETH
Everything is so different, so unbelievable. Even your houses don't look the same.

PIKE
Why, what does your house look like?

ELIZABETH
My house is made from logs that we cut down. It took a long time and it's not even half the size of these. How long did it take you to build your house?

AMBER
Well, I didn't personally build it.

ELIZABETH
You didn't help to make your house? How do you get your homes built before winter if you don't help build it?

GERRIT
We buy the house after someone else makes it. Hardly anyone makes their own house anymore.

ELIZABETH
What do you do if you're not building houses? Do you tend to the land?

PIKE
Look around you. Do you see any land to tend?

ELIZABETH
Where do you get your food then?

SAM
At the store. Don't you have stores?

ELIZABETH
Yes. There's a general store in the village. It sells some food but mostly clothes, tools, candles and other things. We have to grow our own food.

CHELSEA
Don't tell me you just have one store.

ELIZABETH
How many do you have?

CHELSEA
Oh, let me tell you. We have stores for everything now. Like one for food, one for clothes, one for tools, one for books…

AMBER
Except for the superstore. They sell everything.

CHELSEA
And malls. Oh, I love malls. Store after store filled with clothes, and more clothes. I love shopping for clothes. How do you get enough clothes to wear each day of the week if you only have one store?

ELIZABETH
I wear the same dress all week.

CHELSEA gasps.

CHELSEA
You only have one dress?

ELIZABETH
No. I have another one that's for church and good wear.

CHELSEA
Two dresses! Two dresses? I wouldn't know what to do. I'm taking you to the mall.

AMBER
I don't think that's a good idea.

CHELSEA
Why not?

AMBER
Because we need to figure out how to get her home.

PIKE
Why can't she stay here? I want to find out what pioneer boys do. Do they do karate?

PIKE does a quick demonstration.

ELIZABETH
I've never seen a boy do that unless he was poking around in a hornet's nest.

GERRIT
She can't stay. We don't know what will happen to her cellular structure if she stays too long. And she can't see too much because it could change history if she goes back and invents a plane or something.

SAM
If we had actually made it back in time, we could have changed history.

AMBER
We wouldn't have seen anything that people don't already know about.

PIKE
We could build a plane while we're there.

AMBER
In a day? Besides, her parents are going to worry about where she is. She needs to go home as soon as possible.

ELIZABETH
I have to look after my baby sister. If I'm not there Mama can't help the neighbours make quilts for the poor people.

CHELSEA
Aren't you poor?

AMBER
Chelsea! That's not nice.

CHELSEA
Well, she only has two dresses and a small house and no car.

ELIZABETH
We have two rooms in our home, chickens for our eggs, a cow, a horse to pull our buggy and a hundred acres of land. That's better than most folks around us have.

SAM
What about toys? Do you have any?

ELIZABETH
Of course. I have two dolls. I made one of them from fabric pieces that were too small to use for anything else. And I have my own slate so I can draw pictures. And we play lots of games like hopscotch and tag. And my friends and I make decorations for church.

SAM
That's it? What about TV and video games and stuff?

ELIZABETH
I don't know what those things are.

PIKE
Of course, she doesn't, Sam. She probably doesn't even have electricity.

SAM
How do you work on your computer?

GERRIT
How did you qualify to get into the special science class with us? Think. She's from 1868. How could she have any of that stuff?

SAM
Oh yah. I forgot.

AMBER
OK, Elizabeth. I'm going to make some adjustments to the time machine. Why don't you guys show her those things you were talking about? I'll tell you when I'm ready.

Everyone but AMBER goes off to the side. AMBER stays and fiddles with the machine.

PIKE
Do you want to listen to my phone?

ELIZABETH shrugs. PIKE puts his headphones on ELIZABETH'S head and pushes a button. She screams and pulls the head phones off.

ELIZABETH
What was that?

PIKE
That's rap. Why, was it too loud?

AMBER
Are you serious? I can hear it from here. Not everyone listens to music so loud it makes you deaf. Play her something quieter.

PIKE fiddles around with his phone and then hands it back to ELIZABETH. She suspiciously places the headphones back her head and listens for a moment.

ELIZABETH
THIS IS NICE!

She enjoys the music while the others play on their devices.

AMBER
OK. I'm finished.

SAM
Are you sure it works now?

AMBER
Yep. Everything checks out OK.

GERRIT
You said that the last fifteen times.

AMBER
Yes, but this time I am certain it will work.

CHELSEA
You said that the last fifteen times too.

AMBER
It will work.

PIKE
How will we know?

AMBER
If it works, she won't be here anymore.

SAM
But what if she goes somewhere else? Or sometime else?

AMBER
Umm. I guess we will just have to make sure we go back to 1868 and visit her.

AMBER taps on ELIZABETH'S shoulders and she jumps in surprise and pulls the earphones out.

ELIZABETH
These head bun things are great. I wish we had these where I come from.

GERRIT
They're called headphones, and Amber says the machine is working and ready to take you home.

ELIZABETH
Can I take this phone head and music home with me?

PIKE
My mom would kill me if I gave them away. Besides, you need electricity to charge the batteries so it would only be good for a couple of hours. Then it won't work anymore.

ELIZABETH
That's too bad.

AMBER
So, are you ready to go?

ELIZABETH
I suppose so.

CHELSEA
Don't you want to go home?

ELIZABETH
I want to see what else your time has that we don't. And I will miss you.

CHELSEA
We could come visit you.

ELIZABETH
That would be nice. Just don't talk about your time. People might think you're not right in the head.

SAM
Some people think that already.

GERRIT
Speak for yourself.

AMBER
Ok, Elizabeth, step in.

ELIZABETH enters the time machine.

CHELSEA
Bye. It was nice to meet you.

ELIZABETH
It was nice to meet all of you too.

They say goodbye. The machine door is closed. ELIZABETH sneaks out the back without the audience seeing. It shakes and then when it stops AMBER opens the door. It is empty.

AMBER
I guess it works now.

PIKE
Unless you sent her back to a lion pit in ancient civilization somewhere.

CHELSEA
I hope not. She's too nice to be eaten by lions.

AMBER
She will be fine but tomorrow we can go visit her just to make sure.

SAM
Can't we go now?

AMBER
I have to check some things.

PIKE
Why? It must work. Elizabeth's gone.

AMBER
Yes, but I want to make sure we go to the same place she went.

GERRIT
If you haven't changed any of the settings, then in theory we should go to wherever she went.

AMBER
You're right. Ok. Let's go now. I think everything checks out OK.

PIKE, CHELSEA, SAM and GERRIT *all yell*
That's what you said the last sixteen times!

They go into the machine and close the door. Machine starts to shake and make mechanical noises. They sneak behind the machine without the audience seeing them. The door swings open to reveal the machine is empty.

THE END

PRODUCTION NOTES FOR *THE TIME MACHINE*

RUNNING TIME
20 minutes

CHARACTERS
Elizabeth, Pike, Amber, Sam, Gerrit, and Chelsea

COSTUMES
All characters wear regular clothing except for Elizabeth who is dressed in pioneer clothing.

PROPS
A time machine large enough for 6 people to stand in with a back entrance. This can be a large box or two chairs on a table with a sheet over it.
2 cell phones
Headphones
4 chairs
Flashlight
An 'emergency box'—can be an empty tool box that the flashlight fits in
Books or activities for characters to be playing with at the beginning

SET
The garage at Amber's house.

LIGHTING

No special lighting is necessary.
If you wish, you can flash coloured lights when the time machine is working, but is not necessary.

WORKING TOGETHER TO SAVE THE ENVIRONMENT

By Jackie Bennett

STEPHANIE is sitting on her desk. SIMON walks over to STEPHANIE with a piece of folded paper in his hand.

> STEPHANIE
> What did we get Simon? It better be more exciting than the last group assignment.

SIMON unfolds the paper.

> SIMON
> It says, "Make a funny presentation about the environment."

> STEPHANIE
> Are you serious? This is worse than the last one. There's nothing funny about the environment. What are we going to do?

> SIMON
> What about a poster?

> STEPHANIE
> How is that going to get us an A?

> SIMON
> Who cares if we get an A? If I get more than a D my parents will be happy.

> STEPHANIE
> Mine won't. And what's funny about a poster?

> SIMON
> We could make it a comic.

> STEPHANIE
> Mmm. Yah, that might work.

JULIAN approaches STEPHANIE and SIMON.

JULIAN
I don't have a group. Can I be in yours?

STEPHANIE looks at SIMON and shakes her head 'no' without JULIAN seeing them.

SIMON
You can't. We already planned what we're doing.

JULIAN leaves.

STEPHANIE
That was close. I don't like working with him. He never does any work.

SIMON
Yah I know. He just fools around. So, what are we going to make our comic about?

SIMON draws some ideas on a piece of paper until JULIAN returns.

JULIAN
Miss Hester says I have to be in your group cause all the others are full.

SIMON
Aww! Stephanie, go tell Miss Hester we've already started.

STEPHANIE
Why me?

SIMON
Cause she likes you better than me.

STEPHANIE
Fine.

STEPHANIE goes off stage. JULIAN and SIMON glare at each other until STEPHANIE comes back.

STEPHANIE
She says we have to.

SIMON
Great! There goes my C.

JULIAN
I don't wanna be in your group any more.

STEPHANIE
But Miss Hester says you have to.

JULIAN
But you don't want me in your group.

SIMON
That's 'cause you never do any work.

JULIAN
I work.

STEPHANIE
None of us are working at the moment. Let's stop wasting time. We have to make a funny presentation about the environment.

JULIAN
What's funny about the environment?

SIMON
That's what Stephanie said, so I said we should make a poster with a comic about the environment.

JULIAN
That's boring.

STEPHANIE
We already decided before you joined us, so that's what we're doing.

JULIAN
I'm going to make a sculpture out of Popsicle sticks.

SIMON
What's that got to do with our idea?

JULIAN
Nothing, but it's more fun than a poster.

STEPHANIE
If you're going to be in our group, you have to do what we're doing. I'll get a large piece of paper. Julian, can we use your markers?

JULIAN
Maybe.

STEPHANIE gets a large piece of paper, JULIAN gets his markers.

SIMON
OK. So, I am going to draw the pictures. You do the writing.

STEPHANIE.
Your printing is neater.

JULIAN
What about me?

SIMON
You can give us ideas. OK. So, let's do it about pollution.

STEPHANIE
Why pollution?

SIMON
'Cause pollution is hurting the environment and is making the air bad, and clouds of smoke are easy to draw. I can make one big black cloud with everyone choking to death with green slime coming out of their ears.

JULIAN
That's really funny.

STEPHANIE
I don't see what's funny about that.

JULIAN
Exactly. Simon, your idea is not funny.

SIMON
We could make the people clowns. Clowns are funny.

JULIAN
Not if they're dying.

SIMON starts drawing a picture on the large paper. HANNAH walks over.

HANNAH
Miss Hester said I should join your group.

SIMON
Aw. No way. We're full.

STEPHANIE
And we already started.

HANNAH
All the other groups have five people and Miss Hester said yours doesn't.

SIMON
We're finished anyways.

STEPHANIE
That's not fair. She'll get a mark for doing nothing.

SIMON holds up his poster.

Playscripts

SIMON
What do you think?

HANNAH
What is it?

SIMON
It's a funny poster about air pollution.

JULIAN
More like a poster for garbage since that's where it belongs.

SIMON
Thanks a lot. I worked very hard on it.

STEPHANIE
Worked hard? You spent like two minutes on it. We'll be lucky if we even get a D. My parents are going to kill me.

SIMON
Well, I didn't see either of you helping.

JULIAN
You said I couldn't.

SIMON
You were supposed to give ideas. You gave none, so I used none.

JULIAN
Well, here's an idea.

JULIAN rips the poster in half.

SIMON
Julian! I'm telling. Miss Hester! Julian ruined our project.

STEPHANIE
Oh hush. We can just tape it.

HANNAH
The poster didn't make any sense anyway.

SIMON
It makes sense. See? It is, or it was, a funny poster about air pollution. And the clouds are making the clowns cough.

HANNAH
Is that what it was? I thought it was dirty socks covering dead trees.

SIMON
Dirty socks? Dead trees? Are you blind?

JULIAN
You must be blind if you think those dead trees are clowns.

HANNAH
This poster doesn't even say anything. We at least need a title.

JULIAN
How about *Reject Trees*?

SIMON
Stop calling them trees.

JULIAN
Whatever. I'm doing my own picture.

HANNAH
How are we supposed to help the environment when we can't even work together?

STEPHANIE
That's it. We must work together to save the environment.

HANNAH
Yes, but how?

STEPHANIE
No, that's the title for the project.

HANNAH
Mmm. Sounds good to me.

SIMON
I guess, but it doesn't really have anything to do with my picture.

JULIAN
Maybe we need a new picture.

HANNAH
We can still use some of your ideas, Simon, but we need something more.

STEPHANIE
Especially if we're going to get an A.

SIMON
So, what are we going to do?

HANNAH
To start with, your poster doesn't say anything. We need some facts.

SIMON
I don't know any facts.

STEPHANIE
Then we need to find some. Hannah, why don't you look for some in this textbook.

STEPHANIE hands the book to HANNAH.

HANNAH
OK.

HANNAH starts to flip through the book.

STEPHANIE
Simon, you can be in charge of artwork.

JULIAN
What am I going to do?

STEPHANIE
You and I need to think of a way to make the environment funny for our presentation. What could we do?

JULIAN
We could make a structure that has something to do with pollution.

STEPHANIE
Maybe.

JULIAN
Yah, and then we could set it on fire to show the clouds of bad air!

SIMON
And then set off the fire alarm and get us all suspended.

HANNAH
We don't have to do air pollution. There's a list in this book of other problems besides pollution. There's climate change, endangered species, recycling, and garbage.

SIMON
That's not all going to fit on one poster.

HANNAH
We'll have to do something else, like a play. Then we can give lots of information.

JULIAN
How's that going to be funny?

SIMON
We could dress like clowns.

JULIAN
I am not dressing up like a clown.

HANNAH looks up from her book.

HANNAH
Did you know they have to cut down almost 30,000 trees every day so we can have toilet paper?

SIMON
That's impossible. There wouldn't be any trees left.

HANNAH
That's what it says. And every day more animals and plants become extinct because of humans. And here it says some of the stuff they make pesticides from might cause cancer.

JULIAN
This is depressing. There is nothing funny about the environment.

STEPHANIE
Maybe Miss Hester meant talk about the environment in a funny way to make it more interesting so people will listen. Like Simon's comic strip.

SIMON
Or do a clown play.

JULIAN
I am not going to be a clown.

HANNAH
This book also has ideas for how we can make the environment better. We could maybe do a talk show and interview people to talk about different things we shouldn't do and can do.

STEPHANIE
What ideas?

HANNAH
It says to use the same bag when you go shopping instead of getting more plastic ones.

SIMON
My dad already does that when he buys groceries.

HANNAH
And we can grow vegetables.

JULIAN
How does that help the environment? I bet they just put that there to try and make kids eat more vegetables.

HANNAH
It says growing your own vegetables saves trips to the grocery store, which means less gas polluting the air.

SIMON
We could grow a garden for our project.

STEPHANIE
We only have two weeks. It takes months for anything to grow. And whose back yard are we going to grow it in?

JULIAN
And it's winter.

STEPHANIE
And that only shows one part of the environment. We'll probably get a better mark if we talk about different things. What else is in that book?

HANNAH
Have you ever heard of sick building syndrome?

SIMON
Now that's funny. We could draw a picture of a building barfing all over the people walking below it.

JULIAN
Buildings can't barf. They must mean it's sick, like, that's so awesome.

HANNAH
Actually, it's the people in the building who get sick.

SIMON
Then why isn't it called barfing people syndrome?

STEPHANIE
You're making this up. Give me that.

STEPHANIE takes the book from HANNAH.

STEPHANIE
What do you know? It's real. It's because of things in the building like mold or bad ventilation. Hmm. Who would have known?

SIMON
Maybe this school is sick, and we should do our project about closing the building down so we don't have to go to school anymore.

JULIAN
Now that's a great idea.

HANNAH
Except no one is sick so we'd have a hard time proving it.

STEPHANIE
This book is filled with great facts. Did you know we throw out almost three kilos of garbage away every day, each? And almost half of junk mail isn't even opened when it's thrown away? That's true. My mom never opens ours.

HANNAH
That's a lot of garbage.

SIMON
We don't have that much garbage at my house 'cause we recycle. So, I can't see how we can do anything else to help.

STEPHANIE
Here's a way. We use over two million plastic bottles every hour.

They look at the water bottles on their desks.

                    JULIAN

We only have four bottles. There's still two million more bottles out there. What difference would our four make?

                    STEPHANIE

If we use reusable bottles that would help.

                    SIMON

So, let's do a recycling program for our project.

                    STEPHANIE

We need a project that takes less than two weeks to finish. I like Hannah's idea about doing a talk show. Then we could all take turns telling something different about the environment.

                    SIMON

But this is supposed to be funny. How is a talk show funny?

                    HANNAH

We could tell jokes. Or tell funny stories about people who are trying to help the environment.

                    JULIAN

Yah, like that dog that was supposed to be trained to sniff out mold in some man's old house but ate the man's dinner instead.

                    STEPHANIE

That is funny. Can I be the host?

                    HANNAH

I wanted to be the host.

                    STEPHANIE

It was your idea, so OK. I can be a mad scientist who tells why the world is in trouble.

JULIAN
I want to be a garbage man and talk about how we throw out too many things we could be recycling or reusing. I know, I could take our classroom garbage can and dump it out on Miss Hester's desk and show all the things we should have recycled.

HANNAH
That could get disgusting.

SIMON
But funny.

STEPHANIE
Or it could cost us our A.

SIMON
I think it's a good idea, Julian.

HANNAH
Simon, what are you going to do?

SIMON
If we're going to make this funny, there's only one thing I can be. A clown!

JULIAN
Well, you better be a clown who knows something about saving the environment.

SIMON
I will.

HANNAH
What's the name of our show going to be?

STEPHANIE
We already have a title.

SIMON
We do?

JULIAN
Oh yah. We do.

All OF THEM
Working together to save the environment.

HANNAH
Coming soon to a station near you.

THE END

PRODUCTION NOTES FOR *WORKING TOGETHER*

Characters
Simon, Stephanie, Julian, Hannah

Setting
Classroom

Costumes
Regular clothes

Props
Small folded piece of paper with assignment on it
Large piece of paper or Bristol board
Scrap paper for drawing on
Markers
4 plastic bottles of water
A book about the environment

SOURCES

As with all subjects, expectations surrounding drama instruction are covered in curriculum documents issued by provincial ministries and departments of education. These documents have been invaluable in the preparation of this book. Much of the terminology used in this book to discuss key concepts and best practices in teaching drama is also used in the curriculum documents.

Alberta Arts Curriculum
British Columbia Arts Education Curriculum
Foundation for the Atlantic Canada Arts Education Curriculum
Manitoba Drama Curriculum
Quebec Arts Education
Saskatchewan Arts Education Documents
The Ontario Curriculum : The Arts Grade 1–8

www.ingramcontent.com/pod-product-compliance
Lightning Source LLC
Chambersburg PA
CBHW061746070526
44585CB00025B/2813